THE ILLUSTRATED
RAY BRADBURY

Borgo Press Books by JAMES ARTHUR ANDERSON

The Altar: A Novel of Horror

The Illustrated Ray Bradbury: A Structuralist Reading of Bradbury's The Illustrated Man

Out of the Shadows: A Structuralist Approach to Understanding the Fiction of H. P. Lovecraft

THE ILLUSTRATED RAY BRADBURY

A STRUCTURALIST READING OF BRADBURY'S *THE ILLUSTRATED MAN*

JAMES ARTHUR

ANDERSON

THE BORGO PRESS
MMXIII

THE MILFORD SERIES
POPULAR WRITERS OF TODAY
(ISSN 0163-2469)

Volume Seventy-Seven

THE ILLUSTRATED RAY BRADBURY

Copyright © 1990, 2013 by James Arthur Anderson

SECOND EDITION

Published by Wildside Press LLC

www.wildsidebooks.com

DEDICATION

To Lynn Llorye,
who still makes my dreams come true.

CONTENTS

INTRODUCTION 9
CHAPTER ONE: "The Veldt": The Destructive Fantasy 25
CHAPTER TWO: "Kaleidoscope": The Redemptive Fantasy. 63
CHAPTER THREE: "The Long Rain": The Self-Delusional Fantasy 79
CHAPTER FOUR: "Zero Hour": The Destructive Fantasy Revisited 93
CHAPTER FIVE: "The Rocket": The Artistic Fantasy 105
CONCLUSION. 123
WORKS CITED 139
APPENDIX: Dictionary of Symbols 143
CLASSIFICATION of the Stories of *The Illustrated Man* 147
ABOUT THE AUTHOR 151

INTRODUCTION

Ray Bradbury was one of the first science fiction writers to achieve the best of two worlds. His books have sold millions of copies and have remained continually in print, even though science fiction has only recently achieved "best-selling" status. Even more noteworthy, perhaps, Bradbury's works have been accepted as serious literature in an age when science fiction is still burdened by the old stigma of being "pulp" literature. His stories have found their way into anthologies of modern fiction and are frequently taught in college classes.

In this book I intend to examine the Ray Bradbury phenomenon by conducting a structuralist reading of selected short stories from one of his best-known collections, *The Illustrated Man*. This structuralist reading will attempt to illuminate how Bradbury has captured the imagination of the reading public and earned the respect of the academic community. *The Illustrated Man*, originally published in 1951, represents Bradbury at his best. I will use the stories from this collection to illustrate (pardon the pun) Bradbury's narrative techniques and to expose his major literary themes. My analysis of the stories will show that Bradbury cannot be classified as a science fiction writer, at least not in the traditional sense of the term. Finally, I will show that *The Illustrated Man* is more than just a collection of short stories: this analysis will demonstrate that it is a unified work in which each story contributes to the meaning of the collection as a whole.

I have chosen to analyze the stories using a structuralist methodology for several reasons. First, structuralism has always been attracted to popular literature. Early structuralist critics such as V. Propp and Claude Levi-Strauss examined myths and folktales; later structuralists studied detective stories (Todorov, *Poetics* 42-52), as well as science fiction (Scholes, *Fabulation*) and the literature of the fantastic (Todorov, *Fantastic*), stories that, I feel, represent the mythology of the space age. Popular fiction best represents the thoughts and ideas of the culture that produces it, and structuralism defines itself, in part, as cultural analysis that "seeks to explore the relationship between the system of literature and the culture of which it is a part" (Scholes, *Structuralism* 11).

Second, *The Illustrated Man* makes good material for a structuralist reading because the stories are connected to a larger framework that links them together to form an overall theme. We can, therefore, use structuralist techniques (such as Todorov's plot "equations") that compare stories to find a common plot as tools to show relationships between stories in a collection. Finally, structuralism as a critical methodology has historically been used primarily to study prose, most notably, perhaps, short fiction. Traditional formalist techniques concentrate more on theme than method, while structuralists such as Gerard Genette and Seymour Chatman have developed a science of narratology. This study of how a story works, in addition to what it actually says, seems most appropriate for analyzing Bradbury's style and attempting to account for his popular success.

To "illustrate" Bradbury I will use a specific methodology, that of Robert Scholes (*Semiotics* 87-104), which I will adapt to my analysis as needed. This method combines the interpretive techniques of three of the most influential structuralist critics to date: Tzvetan Todorov, Gerard Genette, and Roland Barthes. I will apply this methodology to five stories from *The Illustrated Man*: "The Veldt", "Kaleidoscope", "The Long Rain", "Zero Hour", and "The Rocket", and to the narrative framework, the prologue and epilogue of the work.

I realize that these methods were never intended to be used for the purposes of explication to which I will put them. A "pure" structuralist would never approve of my interpretive technique; however, I feel that these various structuralist theories "complement one another in addressing the fictional text from different angles" (Scholes, *Semiotics* 87), and that they can be used for textual analysis. I will adapt these methods as needed in each particular story, since my goal is an understanding of *The Illustrated Man*, not an essay on structuralist dogma.

The first of these three methods, that of Tzvetan Todorov, catalogues stories according to plot structure by reducing plot to the form of an equation, much like the grammatical diagram of the sentence, where nouns represent characters and verbs represent action. This method allows the critic to reduce stories to their barest form, then to compare them for similar plot structures. Looking at the nouns and verbs of several related stories may afford the critic some unusual insights; often, the reduction process forces the critic to thematize the work in novel and productive ways. Although Todorov's ultimate aim is to catalogue all the plots that occur in literature, his critical method can be quite valuable, I think, in the analysis of a single collection of related texts.

The second critical method I will use is that of Gerard Genette. Genette's narrative theory distinguishes between narrative and discourse. The narrative, or "story", includes the basic sequence of events that occurs in the text. The discourse refers to the way that the author tells the story. To use this method of analysis, the critic examines narrative voice, time reference and frequency, and the pace of actual events in the story. The critic looks at narrative voice in order to determine who narrates the story and through whose point of view the events are seen. This structuralist study goes beyond mere "point of view" to determine how and why a narrative may subtly shift from one focus character to another. The critic examines the time reference and frequency to isolate the present narrative from the past, as shown in flashbacks, and from the future, as shown in foreshadowing and predictions. Finally, the critic looks at the speed with which the discourse moves through the sequence of events in the story.

The third critical method is that of Roland Barthes as outlined in *S/Z*. Barthes examines a text by breaking it down into a series of semiotic "codes" common to all literature. In order to understand anything, be it a work of literature, a piece of music, or an advertisement on television, the human mind must interpret it through fixed codes of understanding. Language itself represents such a code; unless one understands the "code of English," discourse in English becomes meaningless. According to Barthes, there are five basic codes of understanding in any artistic work. These are the proairetic code (or code of actions), the hermeneutic code (or code of enigmas), the cultural code, the connotative code, and the symbolic code:

> ...Each code is one of the forces that can take over the text (of which the text is the network), one of the voices out of which the text is woven. Alongside each utterance, one might say that the off-stage voices can be heard: they are the codes: in their interweaving, these voices... de-originate the utterance: the convergence of the voices (of the code) becomes *writing*, a stereographic space where the five codes, the five voices, intersect.... (*S/Z* 21)

In addition, written works may contain a textual code, and a specialized symbolic code called the psychoanalytical code.

The first two codes, the action and hermeneutic codes, define the narrative elements that distinguish between the story and the discourse. The action code resembles the grammatical diagram of Todorov, or the "story" of Genette, except that it concentrates more on the physical actions of the story—Todorov's "verbs" in the plot sentence. Since I will be applying the theories of Todorov and Genette in my analysis, I will focus on Barthes' action code primarily in terms of the physical location and movement of the plot's actions (i.e. outside to inside; down to up). The hermeneutic code, or "code of enigmas," reveals the series of questions or puzzles that an author uses to create suspense in a story. The reader desires answers to these puzzles, yet the author withholds this information until the last possible moment. This code is especially important in popular fiction—indeed, the detective story finds its sole *raison d'être* in the code of enigmas. This code, again, overlaps some of Genette's work and will be used only occasionally in my analysis.

The last three codes, the cultural, connotative, and symbolic codes, work together to create character, enhance meaning, and determine theme in a literary work. The cultural code examines the literary work's explicit and implicit references to the culture in which it was written. Understanding this code enables the reader to view the work as being the product of a particular culture and society, and may expose themes and meaning deemed important by that particular culture. The connotative code schematizes the dominant connotations of the text's language in regard to character and setting. This code often develops character in traditional stories; in science fiction (and most popular literature), where plot is more important than character, the connotative code often contributes primarily to the work's overall theme. Finally, the symbolic code assumes that meaning occurs through binary oppositions that create theme through their conflict. The psychoanalytical code, for example, is a specialized symbolic code based on Freud's theories.

Barthes' textual code, or metalinguistic code, operates whenever communication speaks of itself—as when a poet writes a poem about poetry, for example. This code occurs whenever "...language is...doubled into two layers of which the first in some ways cap the second...." (Barthes, "Valdemar" 139). This textual code will often expose themes dealing with writing or communication.

Barthes uses his codes to interpret specific literary works (*S/Z*, "Valdemar") by dividing the text into random units that he terms "lexias" (*S/Z* 13) and picking the codes out of each fragmented section. For purposes of my analysis, however, I will not fragment the text, but will demonstrate how the five codes weave their way through the work as a whole.

I intend to use the perspectives of Genette, coupled with Barthes' hermeneutic and action codes to show how Bradbury has achieved popular success through his ability to create and maintain suspense while keeping the story moving quickly towards its conclusion. This analysis will show how Bradbury uses ellipsis to move quickly from one scene to another in cinematic fashion. I will also demonstrate how Bradbury uses analepses and prolepses to distribute clues to the story's ending throughout the text and how he produces surprise endings by changing the narrative focus at critical points in the discourse.

Todorov's ideas on genre can be adduced to suggest that Bradbury should not be classified as a "science fiction" writer at all, since his stories do not fall into a strict science fiction format but have pioneered a new subgenre that rests midway between fantasy and science fiction. When he does base his plot on scientific principles, these are often the laws of psychology and sociology rather than those of chemistry or physics. And even this science is often tempered with fantasy or magic. This marriage of genres has enabled Bradbury to create a more literary type of science-fantasy and has molded speculative fiction into the complex and virtually unclassifiable genre that it is today.

Todorov's "equations" are also helpful in isolating

specific themes in the stories, which I will then examine in more detail by using Barthes' connotative, symbolic, psychoanalytical, and cultural codes. In particular, we will find oppositions between fantasy and reality, childhood and adulthood, primitiveness and civilization, and creation and destruction repeated in each of the stories. Also, a "code of ambiguity" will emerge that foregrounds structural or thematic uses of irony and reversal.

Finally, I will show that *The Illustrated Man* contains a textual code that links together the themes from each story. The bipolar oppositions from each story (fantasy/reality, etc.), when woven together in terms of the code of ambiguity and the textual code, create a rich tapestry of meaning that can only be seen once all the stories have been read and understood within the context of the narrative framework for the collection as a whole.

It is necessary here to give a brief synopsis of this framework. The narrator, a young man, is walking along a deserted country road when he meets the Illustrated

Man. The Illustrated Man tells his new friend a strange story about his tattoos—the pictures come alive and tell the future. Fascinated, the young man listens, then as the Illustrated Man falls asleep, he watches the pictures move and come to life. Each illustration tells one of the stories in the collection. Once the narrator has witnessed all of the tales told by the illustrations and has learned each of their individual lessons, he looks at the one blank spot on the Illustrated Man's back. There he sees an image of himself beginning to form, becoming real, and this new illustration shows the Illustrated Man strangling him. The narrator runs away before the last picture crystallizes, before it can become real. Thus, he changes the reality predicted by the illustration and escapes with his life.

The narrator has experienced the lessons or themes that each of the stories tells, just as the reader will experience these themes as he reads the stories. He will witness the destructive power of fantasy and imagination in "The Veldt" and "Zero Hour," and thus learn how our primitive wishes may lead to catastrophe if they are allowed to become reality. He will observe the redemptive power of fantasy in "Kaleidoscope" and learn how the child's belief can actually create or redeem life when based upon hope and innocent wonder. Finally, he will witness the artistic power of fantasy when the child's boundless imagination is tempered with adult knowledge and control, and when this power is put to constructive purposes.

By putting these various lessons together, our narrator learns an overall truth: fantasy can become reality through imagination, and this fantasy may either be a destructive or a constructive force, depending upon its use. The child is born with the ability to imagine, yet he lacks the knowledge to control and channel this talent. As he grows older, the adult loses the ability to imagine, even as he gains the knowledge necessary to use his imagination. If the adult can retain his child-like ability to imagine, and if he has the knowledge to use it wisely, he will be able to make fantasy become real by channeling his talent into some form of artistic communication.

The narrator of *The Illustrated Man* learns to believe in the power of fantasy by watching the pictures on the tattooed man's back. He learns to believe in the possibility of fantasy becoming real, and he learns of the potential dangers of this genesis. He saves himself by learning this important lesson and realizes that the Illustrated Man lacks the knowledge to control his own fantastic illustrations. Thus, the narrator escapes from a destructive fantasy and learns to use his own child-like imagination by narrating the tales of *The Illustrated Man* to an audience to become a creative artist in his own right. His telling of the stories brings fantasy to life for the reader as the narrator creates the tales on the printed page. The entire collection of stories serves as a warning to the reader—and society—that we must not become too adult to imagine, nor remain too childish to understand. Otherwise, either we will be uncreative, or else our creations will ultimately destroy us. And for Bradbury, who wrote these tales during the height of the cold war and nuclear arms race, our artistic creations may involve technology that can be highly destructive.

CHAPTER ONE
"THE VELDT": THE DESTRUCTIVE FANTASY

The first story of *The Illustrated Man*, a disquieting tale entitled "The Veldt," immediately follows the prologue of the collection and represents the first of the illustrations coming to life to narrate a tale. "The Veldt" was originally written in 1950, and has been widely anthologized, most notably in *The Norton Anthology of Short Fiction* (edited by R. V. Cassill), a popular text in college literature courses. This first story is perhaps the most complex in the entire collection in regard to theme; however "The Veldt" achieved popular success long before it achieved literary success. A look at the techniques used in this story to create and maintain narrative suspense demonstrates why *The Illustrated Man* has sold millions of copies in an age when few people read. Genette's science of narratology and Barthes' action codes are particularly effective methods for examining the functions and effects of such narrative suspense.

The central point of Genette's theory is to make the distinction between story and discourse, the former consisting of the series of events that compose the plot, the latter referring to the manner in which the author narrates the story. Genette's theory recognizes that literary texts are seldom written in strict chronological order, but move backward and forward in time from the "present" (base time) of the narrative. His concept of prolepsis and analepsis illustrates this narrative technique.

Most modern short stories do not begin at the beginning, but begin somewhere toward the end, then fill in the beginning and back-story with flashbacks, or analepses, which Genette defines as "any evocation after the fact of an event that took place earlier than the point in the story where we are at any given moment" (*Narrative* 40). Strictly speaking, the story of "The Veldt" begins when George and Lydia first buy their new home—their troubles begin at that point. The discourse, however, begins a year later, when the parents first become aware of the changes in their children. The narrative provides needed background through analepses. On page 7, for example (all page numbers refer to the 1969 Bantam edition), the technology of the Happy-life home is explained, and a reference is made to the purchase of the home, an event that occurred before the discourse begins. On page 9 another analepsis refers to Peter's being punished a month earlier: "When I punished him a month ago by locking the nursery for even a few hours—the tantrum he threw!" (This sentence, of course, serves as a prolepsis as well, since it foreshadows the ending of the story). Bradbury uses an analepsis to mention another past event: "They've been acting funny ever since you forbade them to take the rocket to New York a few months ago" (13).

Bradbury employs these analepses for two distinct

purposes. First, they efficiently fill in needed background and detail, as in the case of the function of the Happy-life home. This allows Bradbury to begin his narrative at a crucial point of story time—at a point where the action is about to reach a crisis that will quickly lead to the story's climax. Secondly, the analepses provide the reader with "clues" to the story's resolution. Thus, the children's anger at having the nursery turned off earlier will recur at the end. This anger and their anger at not being allowed to take the rocket to New York will explain their present behavior and motivate their future actions.

Most popular short stories in the mystery, horror, and science fiction genres depend upon a surprise or unusual ending for their mass appeal. Yet the ending cannot be too much of a surprise—enough clues must be planted throughout the story so that the reader can understand how the "surprise" ending came about. Otherwise the reader feels cheated, feels that the author was not playing fair since there was no possibility of anticipating the ending. The prolepsis, or foreshadowing device, plants clues within the narrative. Some of these clues, as we have seen, may be analepses, events from the past that take on significance in the future. Other clues will not be related to the past.

"The Veldt" contains a number of prolepses that foreshadow the tale's outcome. On page 7, in the fourth line of the story, Lydia mentions calling in a psychologist to look at the nursery. This, of course, intimates the psychological problems of the children, and of their society in general. Bradbury follows this initial clue with others that refer to psychology. On page 10 George thinks: "They were awfully young, Wendy and Peter, for death thoughts. Or, no, you were never too young, really. Long before you knew what death was you were wishing it on someone else." The children of this society, however, have found the technology to make their wishes come true—even death wishes. Lydia says: "I'm beginning to be sorry we bought that room for the children. If children are neurotic at all, a room like that—" (13). This psychological clue allows the reader to fill in the blank, so to speak, with the worst possible scenario, which is exactly what occurs at the end of the story.

Physical objects can also be used as proleptic clues to the story's outcome. On pages 8-9 the lions appear, a symbol of primitiveness and death. Vultures complement the lions as a death symbol and their shadows foreshadow George's death: "A Shadow passed through the sky. The shadow flickered on George Hadley's upturned, sweating face." This same shadow reappears on page 19: "A shadow flickered over Mr. McClean's hot face. Many shadows flickered." Since Bradbury used the shadow as a prolepsis to anticipate George's death, the reader can assume that McClean's days are numbered if he attempts to interfere with the children's African game.

Another set of physical clues appears on page 13 when George finds his old wallet. "There were drops of saliva on it, it had been chewed, and there were blood smears on both sides." On page 17, George finds a bloody scarf that belonged to Lydia. And each time he enters the veldt land, George hears screams that sound familiar. These clues all point to the story's climax, when George and Lydia are devoured by the lions and realize that the screams they have previously heard were their own.

Genette's division between story and discourse, and especially the foregrounding of prolepsis and analepsis as part of the discourse, helps the critic see how an author creates suspense by beginning his plot at a crucial point, then sprinkling cryptic clues throughout the narrative, which anticipate the ending. Roland Barthes' hermeneutic code offers a slightly different viewpoint on how an author creates suspense by presenting a series of puzzles and enigmas that intrigue readers, yet keep them wondering about the story's outcome. Some enigmas are explained early in the text, as they are essential to the story. Others are not resolved until the very end.

"The Veldt" begins with an enigma; in the second sentence George asks what is wrong with the nursery. Lydia could easily have told him, but this would not have made for a suspenseful discourse. Instead, she shows him the problem. This takes narrative time and keeps the reader interested, since the answer to this enigma is delayed until the sixth paragraph.

Bradbury introduces other enigmas early in the story. Even before the first question is answered, the reader begins wondering about the society of this imaginary world. When the "nursery" is described, the society becomes more puzzling—what kind of world would have a three-dimensional nursery that creates fantasy worlds? The narrator relates information in bits and does not entirely explain this society until page 8 (14th paragraph).

Another enigma appears early in the story when the parents wonder what the lions are eating, and why the screams sound so familiar. The pieces to this puzzle are scattered like clues to a detective story—George finds an old wallet, then a bloodstained handkerchief—but the complete answer does not appear until the last page: "And suddenly they realized why those other screams had sounded familiar." After this realization, the mystery is solved.

Another enigma, though a more subtle one, is posed on page 16 when George asks the psychologist if the lions could become real. The good doctor assures him they could not. In a fantasy story, however, anything can (and usually does) happen, despite the laws of science. The very fact that George even considers such impossibility points to an ending where anything can happen.

In order for a story to gain popular appeal it must move quickly and maintain the reader's interest. "The Veldt" certainly fulfills this criterion. Genette's theory of narrative speed helps us to understand how Bradbury keeps his plot moving forward while stopping in crucial moments to maintain suspense. In addition, Bradbury's use of short, quick scenes gives his stories a cinematic quality popular with modern audiences.

Genette speaks of four speeds of narrative movement: the ellipsis, where time is infinitely rapid; the summary, where time is relatively rapid; the scene, where time is slow; and the pause, where time stands still (*Narrative* 95). The ellipsis can be a traditional transition, such as "three days later...", or it may be a more subtle transition that jumps across a vast period of time, as when an author omits a period of time between chapters without directly telling the reader. The summary also moves the narrative quickly through time, but contains more description than the ellipsis (such as on page 10 of "The Veldt": "they ate dinner alone, for Wendy and Peter were at a special plastic carnival across town...."). The ellipsis and summary connect scenes. The scene, a more detailed minute-to-minute account of the action, attempts to recreate "real" time. Finally, the pause slows down time by describing people, places, or things without actually contributing to the forward motion of the plot. Pauses usually complement scenes by slowing down the action and delaying the resolution in order to create suspense. Important information may be conveyed by pauses while the reader waits to see what will happen next.

"The Veldt" begins with a scene in base time, the

narrative present of the discourse, as George and Lydia discuss the problems with the nursery. The scene lasts for only 12 lines before a summary transports the pair to the nursery itself: "They walked down the hall of their soundproofed, Happylife Home...." (6). A descriptive pause delays the answer to the riddle of what is wrong with the nursery, and fills in important information about the home itself, "...which had cost them thirty thousand dollars installed...." (6). Pauses describe the veldt in realistic detail—"The hot straw smell of the lion grass, the cool green smell of the hidden water hole..." (8)—then the scene resumes as the lions bolt at George and Lydia.

The scene continues through page 9 as Bradbury uses dialogue as a type of descriptive pause to fill in background material:

> "You've got to tell Wendy and Peter not to read any more on Africa."
> "Of course—of course." He patted her.
> "Promise?"
> "Sure."

"And lock the nursery for a few days until I can get my nerves settled."

"You know how difficult Peter is about that. When I punished him a few months ago by locking the nursery for even a few hours—the tantrum he threw! And Wendy too. They live for the nursery" (9).

Instead of summarizing past events or describing them through the narrator's voice, Bradbury allows the characters to speak of the past—the flashbacks are, in effect, handled through dialogue as we learn that the children have been reading about Africa, and throwing tantrums when they fail to get their own way. This technique allows the scene to continue the forward progress of time while filling in past events.

On page 10 Bradbury uses an ellipsis to teleport into the next scene. In fact, five ellipses occur in a story of only thirteen pages. This rapid movement of time keeps the scenes short and tight, and allows Bradbury to ignore events that are unimportant to the narrative. Since plot forms the most important element of science fiction short stories, Bradbury uses the ellipsis to keep the plot moving toward its climax without needless digression or description. This quick movement, combined with flashbacks and a beginning that occurs close to the story's climax allows the author to efficiently condense a year's worth of plot into a mere thirteen pages. The short, quick scenes connected by ellipses resemble scenes from a film where the camera cuts from one scene to the next. Bradbury's cinematic sense makes his stories highly successful in a visually-oriented society like ours, and it is no accident that Bradbury enjoyed success as a scriptwriter (his 1956 script of *Moby Dick* is considered his best), and that several of his works have made the transition to the movies (*Fahrenheit 451*, *Something Wicked this Way Comes*, and, of course, *The Illustrated Man*).

Genette's study of narrative focus fits quite nicely into our discussion of ellipses when we examine the final ellipsis of "The Veldt" (page 19, between the first and second paragraphs). Genette's theory hinges on the fact that a story does not always maintain a consistent narrative focus throughout the discourse; even within a single "point of view" the narrative focus may experience subtle changes from one character to another. Barthes determines the narrative focus of a third-person story by changing the "he" of each of the characters into an "I" (*Image* 112). The narrative focus resides with the character who adjusts to this change without affecting the story's meaning.

Even though Bradbury uses a third person omniscient narrator, George represents the viewpoint character throughout most of "The Veldt"; changing "How many times in the last year had he opened the door and found Wonderland..." to "How many times had I opened the door..." shows that we see the world through George's eyes. After the final ellipsis, however, this test for narrative focus no longer works, since George was killed just before the transition in time. This ellipsis marks not only a change in time, but also a change in narrative focus; the voice subtly shifts from George to an omniscient narrator.

This shift in focus is almost a trademark of Bradbury's

whenever he uses a "trick" or surprise ending, and we will see it again in "Kaleidoscope" and "Zero Hour." This technique enhances the surprise ending in several ways. First, it allows the narrative to cut away from the graphic details of the parents' death, leaving the horror to the reader's imagination. Second, it permits the story to continue after the death of the protagonist. The last paragraph of the story gives the reader some time to realize the horrible implications of the parents' death, and to think about what the children might do to the psychologist. Finally, the change in focus allows Bradbury to focus his narrative through the viewpoint of a character who does not know how the story will end, while still using an omniscient point of view. By using this technique, which Genette terms "paralipsis" (*Narrative* 95), Bradbury can withhold certain information from the reader that the omniscient narrator would know.

We have seen the use of paralipsis before as the omniscient narrator withholds information that would reveal the ending too soon—such as what the lions are eating, for example. This technique works with prolepses, analepses, and Barthes hermeneutic code to create suspense and make the ending effective.

So far I have focused primarily on how Bradbury has created a "marketable" commodity for today's science fiction reader. Yet, although Bradbury's publisher has billed him as "the world's greatest science fiction writer," he does not write true science fiction, at least not in the classical sense. Instead, he has combined science fiction with fantasy, and even with supernatural horror to create a new genre that is neither science fiction nor fantasy, but something in between. I will apply the genre theories of Todorov to "The Veldt" to demonstrate this idea.

Tzevetan Todorov has divided fantastic literature into subgenres—the uncanny and the marvelous (*Fantastic* 41-57). In the uncanny, the unexplained has a logical explanation and this subgenre could be called "the supernatural explained" (44). A tale such as Poe's "The Black Cat" would fall into such a category; the cat is not really a "ghost," but its screech can be logically explained by its being accidentally walled up with the body of the narrator's wife. At the other end of the spectrum, Todorov describes the "marvelous" as a story where the supernatural has no logical explanation (52). A novel such as Stephen King's *'Salem's Lot*, in which vampires take over a small Maine town, is an example of the marvelous.

The "fantastic" lies midway between the marvelous and the uncanny, and represents a story that leaves the reader torn between a logical and a supernatural explanation, and unable to decide which of these two forces are at work. A novel such as *A Turn of the Screw* by Henry James is an example of a "fantastic" novel. These subgenres can be divided further. Todorov feels that modern science fiction falls into the subgenre of the "instrumental marvelous," where the supernatural is "explained in a rational manner, but according to laws which contemporary science does not acknowledge" (*Fantastic* 56). H.P. Lovecraft's "The Colour out of Space" and other tales in his Cthulhu Mythos cycle explain that supernatural "demons" are really aliens from Yuggoth, the planet beyond Neptune, for example.

Todorov's divisions help to explain fantasy, supernatural horror, and science fiction, each of which would be classified as a subgenre of the marvelous. Science fiction uses science, fantasy uses magic, and horror uses forces of the supernatural to explain the impossible. In Bradbury's stories, elements of each of these subgenres appear and overlap to give us a tale that cannot be put in a convenient pigeonhole.

"The Veldt," for example, certainly uses technology to help explain the behavior of the characters of the future society. Yet no amount of science can explain how the children's fantasy veldt turns into a reality. Even the psychologist, an inhabitant of this society who would be familiar with its technology, tells George that the lions could not become real. Yet the children's creative powers somehow transcend technology and enter the realm of magic, an evil magic that borders on the supernatural. The story, then, is not pure science fiction, nor is it pure fantasy since the "magic" involved relies more on psychology than magic wands; furthermore, the ending weaves an element of horror into the science fiction-fantasy tapestry.

Bradbury is usually not thought of as a writer of horror, but he does use the supernatural to give a twist to his "science" fiction (the prologue to *The Illustrated Man* implies that a witch was responsible for the Illustrated Man's tattoos). His is a subtle version of horror, however. Unlike many horror writers who graphically depict violence, Bradbury uses the classical technique of allowing the horror and violence to occur offstage. This can be shown by examining "The Veldt" through Barthes' action code.

Barthes' action code details the action of the story—how the plot actually moves the story from beginning to end. In this respect, it resembles both Todorov's diagram and Genette's distinction between story and discourse. Barthes' code goes one step further, however, and also examines the physical situation of the action—how, when, and where it occurs.

Applying the code to "The Veldt," we find two major

actions occurring in the story—the creation of the African veldt, and the destruction of George and Lydia. These actions occur virtually simultaneously on page 18; the lions come to life and immediately take the life of the parents. Yet the creation of the veldt actually begins much earlier, before the discourse begins. And, interestingly enough, the parents are killed "offstage" on page 18-19. Their screams are heard, but the actual description of their death is left to the reader's imagination. As we have seen, this horrible scene is cut off by an ellipses that changes narrative focus.

Bradbury uses horror as part of the action code, yet he uses it in such a subtle way that the reader is often not aware he is reading a horror story. As horror writer T. E. D. Klein explains: "Because it gains power from playing on the reader's imagination, the horror tale is most effective when it suggests instead of spelling out." Offstage horror, such as having George and Lydia killed offstage, is a characteristic of Bradbury that we will see again in "Kaleidoscope" and "Zero Hour," and that occurs throughout his novels in *Something Wicked this Way Comes* and *Murder is a Lonely Business*, for example.

Modern science fiction in its attempt to become "serious literature" has become more and more thematic as the genre has progressed from the early Buck Rogers adventure stories to the complex modern tales of writers such as Ursula K. LeGuin and Frank Herbert. Many of the early stories of Ray Bradbury, written for pulp magazines like *Weird Tales*, *Planet Stories*, and *Thrilling Wonder* in the 1940s, transcend the typical "weird" story that was popular at the time and paved the way for a new generation of speculative writers who combine theme, style, and science fiction. As Timothy Perrin notes:

> Bradbury's stories changed the nature of the market. His horror stories, written for $15, $25, and $35 for *Weird Tales*, are now Gothic classics. The magazines that wouldn't publish Bradbury's new style of human science fiction died and the entire genre adjusted to make room for it ("Nostalgia" 29).

Looking at "The Veldt" through Todorov's method of diagramming the story as a grammatical "equation" will highlight its richly thematic structure. Since a "true" diagram of the complexities of this ambiguous tale would be unnecessarily complicated and confusing, I have taken the liberty of producing a simplified version:

C- opt R> C opt F> C cre F> A opt des F> F bec R> F des A> C bec A> C opt R

where:

A= adult	-=negation of trait	opt=wants
C= child	>=leads to	cre=creates
F= fantasy	bec=becomes	
R= reality	des=destroys	

Todorov's diagram offers the critic a way of representing a story's plot, which he can then compare with other plots. The diagram also illustrates the structuralist's way of isolating bipolar operations. The conflict between two opposing poles creates theme. Fantasy opposes reality; childhood opposes adulthood. These same oppositions will appear again in diagrams of the remaining stories from the Bradbury collection, and will prove to be important to an understanding of *The Illustrated Man* as a whole.

Translating this diagram into English gives the basic story: the children do not like reality; therefore, they create a fantasy in their nursery. The adults, who are quite content with their reality, do not like the children's fantasy (interestingly enough, they do not like it because it is *too* real). The adults want to destroy the children's fantasy and replace it with a more acceptable one (which is less real). The children destroy the adults rather than lose their realistic fantasy. To do this they make their fantasy *become* reality, and this reality destroys the adults. In essence, the children have created reality and, as a consequence, have become adults who are happy with their own reality. The children refuse to grow up; yet this refusal forces them to create their own world and thereby become adults.

One important facet of Todorov's theory concerns the

first and last elements in the equation, which, according to Scholes, should be either equal or opposite: "... what makes the sequence a story is a return to the opening proposition at the end. Stories are about successful or unsuccessful transformation of attributes" (*Semiotics* 89). For example, a character lacking happiness must either achieve happiness, or remain unhappy. Or, in the case of "The Veldt," characters who desire a fantasy ultimately achieve their wish.

The theme of reality vs. fantasy is obvious in this simple diagram. Once the children destroy the adults, fantasy becomes reality. This raises some far-reaching implications and some interesting questions that Bradbury deliberately leaves unanswered: can man create his own reality? Exactly what is reality? Whose reality is the correct one?

The diagram, like a grammatical sentence, is composed of nouns and verbs. The verbs "create", "become", and "destroy" underscore the fantasy/reality theme. The characters, particularly the children, resemble gods who create, destroy, and become.

The adults have created a mechanical universe that has mastered them, and the children have created a universe of their own and made themselves masters of it, or so they believe. The nouns of the equation point out another interesting theme—one that will arise again from the psychological perspective—namely, the theme of adulthood vs. childhood. The children's fantasy seems more real that the adults' reality. It is difficult to differentiate the children from the adults in this story. The adults often act like children, and the children control the adults. Then, of course, when the children become adults at the end of the story they act like the childish adults their parents were as they casually ask the psychologist to tea.

The kind of diagramming suggested by Todorov exposes the various themes or codes of fantasy/reality, childhood/adulthood, and ambiguity. We can explore these themes in more detail using the semiotic codes elaborated by Barthes, especially what he calls the connotative and symbolic codes.

Barthes' connotative code examines how connotations are carried on throughout a story to create specific images that link together to give meaning. In many stories these connotations are a prime ingredient in character development; in "The Veldt", however, where characterization is minimal, they are particularly important in the creation of theme.

Several connotative codes weave their way through "The Veldt." Throughout the work, Bradbury employs words connoting either civilization or the primitive. One example of this is the use of color. Bradbury paints the primitive world of the lions in vivid, real-life colors: the sun is "hot yellow" (7), the parents smell the "cool green smell of the hidden water hole" (8). The lions are the "yellow of an exquisite French tapestry" (8) with "terrible green-yellow eyes" (9). The children's Africa is created with "supersensitive color film" (9) in vivid yellows and greens, complete with three-dimensional sounds and smells. The real world of the adults, however, is painted only with light and darkness, never with color. The Happy-life Home automatically "sensitized a switch somewhere and the nursery light flicked on when they came within ten feet of it" (7). The walls are "crystalline" until the African fantasy appears. This real world, with its absence of color, is a world of chrome, steel, and plastic, an almost make-believe, dream-like world. In contrast, we find the bright, realistic colors of the fantasy world, a nightmare that will, indeed become real at the end of the story.

Another interesting connotative code results from Bradbury's use of living connotations to represent non-living things. The house is depicted as a mother that "fed them and rocked them to sleep and played and sang and was good to them" (7). The house, the most "living" character in the story, was not constructed but "conceived" (8); the nursery was "a miracle" (8)—of birth? Lydia complains that the house is a "wife and mother now and nursemaid" (10), and the psychologist explains that the nursery has become the children's mother and father (16). When the house is turned off, it is "killed" (17) and becomes a "mechanical cemetery" (17) full of the "dead bodies" (17) of machines. At one point George admits "we've been contemplating our mechanical, electronic navels for too long" (17). The house, the adults' fantasy of technology, has become a real, living entity that will destroy them. Meanwhile, the children's primitive fantasy has also become real, and destructive. The adults, who do not realize how their technological fantasy has already weakened them to the point of inaction, cannot recognize the destructive power of the uncontrolled, creative imaginations of their children, imaginations that can transcend science to control technology with primitive, primeval forces that can only be termed "magic."

A third and perhaps more simple connotative code involves the names that Bradbury gives his characters. The characters' names were not chosen by chance, but augment the themes of the story. "Wendy" and "Peter" obviously refer to the characters in *Peter Pan*, a tale about children who refuse to grow up. Wendy and Peter, like their namesakes in the children's story, live in a make-believe fantasy world instead of the "real" world. In *Peter Pan*, the violent fantasies of the children are domesticated; in "The Veldt," however, these fantasies take over and the domestic technology turns violent. Bradbury's tale, then, can be seen almost as a twentieth century parody of the older fantasy story.

Other names used in "The Veldt" have interesting, if less thematic, connotations. The psychologist, aptly named "McClean," expects to clean the children's minds of their death thoughts and brainwash them into accepting the reality of the adults. And, of course, we have the parents last name, "Hadley." These people, indeed, "had" everything they ever wanted or needed, and actually lived for their possessions. Their fantasy of having all of the newest technology became real for them, and destroyed them.

Barthes' symbolic code refers to a diametric opposition between two vital elements of a story and is especially useful in thematizing a work. In the case of "The Veldt," the symbolic code exposes a theme of ambiguity. The nouns and verbs of Todorov's equation seem to become reversed in this story, and traits become switched as fantasy becomes reality and children become adults. Fantasy, reality, childhood, adulthood, and social roles all become confused, profoundly tangled in an intricate web of ambiguity that often leaves the reader wondering what is real and what is not.

Thus, the children become adult—yet, adults act like children, and children act like adults. Fantasy is usually associated with childhood and primitiveness, and reality with civilization and adulthood, yet this association is also laced with an ambiguity that complicates matters. The adults' world is, after all, a fantasy of technology that has become real, and this world seems like a fantasy to the contemporary reader, while the children's African fantasy seems intensely real. In fact, the veldt seems far too real to the adult characters in the story: "This is a little *too* real" (8), and that is why they do not like it. Thus, the adults also live in a fantasy of their own as they hide from the world of their mechanical home, protected from work, pressure, and danger.

The children, in order to escape from their fantastic-reality, invent a realistic fantasy complete with danger—and death. They live closer to reality than their parents, and when their fantasy actually becomes real, they become like their parents, for they, too, have created a fantastic reality, even though it is a primitive world of death rather than a peaceful world of technology. The veldt-land fantasy, like the adults' technology, will protect the children from external reality, including those who threaten to take their fantasy away. In trying to avoid becoming like their parents, the children, paradoxically, have become like them, only in a more violent, primitive manner.

The code of ambiguity, or code of inversion, is actually a kind of symbolic code, a by-product of Todorov's verbs "create" and "destroy." In Bradbury's world, things must often be destroyed in order for other things to be created. This leads to paradoxical inversions—such as children who make fantasy become reality by destroying the parents, who have created a technological fantasy of their own that allows the children to create their own fantasy, which, with the help of some child-like "magic," gives the children the means to destroy them and create a new reality. This code not only highlights the ironies of the situation, but attempts to account for the paradox of "magic" by placing it within a universe of paradoxes.

Examining the story through another symbolic code, the psychoanalytical code, brings us to the concept of Freud's "pleasure principle." This code exposes a major theme in the story by contrasting two symbolic oppositions, childhood and adulthood, and relating them to the previously discussed opposition of fantasy and reality.

According to Freud's theory, the child desires nothing except pleasure and gratification. The adult learns to abandon this search for pleasure and channel it into constructive pursuits such as work, education, or artistic creation. In "The Veldt," not only the children but the whole adult society have become slaves to pleasure. Technology has created a society that no longer needs to work or to create. The children need not paint pictures; they have a machine to create for them. When George shut the machine off so his son could learn how to paint for himself, Peter "didn't like it" (14). "I don't want to do anything but look and listen and smell; what else is there to do?" (14). The children have never learned to channel their energies into creative pursuits.

The adults, of course, are no better. They act like children with nothing to do except have the house, their surrogate mother, wait upon them. They cannot discipline their children; Wendy and Peter eat strawberry ice cream and hot dogs instead of their supper (14), and defy their parents when ordered to eliminate Africa from the nursery. On page 15, Peter even threatens his father: "I don't think you'd better consider it any more, Father." In such an abnormal society, children could not be expected to mature normally.

Structuralism, unlike some "close reading" methods, does not ignore the cultural context of literature. One aim of structuralism is to "explore the relationships between the system of literature and the culture of which it is a part" (Scholes, *Structuralism* 11). Barthes' cultural code illustrates this view nicely by showing that no piece of literature can be entirely divorced from the society that produced it. The cultural code of "The Veldt" cannot be pinned down if the critic looks for cultural codes of the future. This code has its basis in the society that produced the work, and in the society in which it is read, and not necessarily in the society depicted in the story. Science fiction, in particular, finds it difficult, if not impossible, to create a totally "alien" society, or a society completely of the future. Instead it must rely upon cultures that are already known and project them into the future.

"The Veldt" demonstrates the culture of modern America, not that of some undefined future. The primary cultural code concerns idleness and its association with Freud's "pleasure principle," which has already been discussed. This code comments negatively on modern society by illustrating what will happen if it persists unchanged. (Science fiction writers commonly use this "what if" device to generate story ideas.) Bradbury envisions that we would live in a world like that depicted in "The Veldt" if the technology were available to make the fantasy happen. While Bradbury may have been expressing reservations about the rapid development of television in the 1950s, it is worth noting that in the decades since the publication of this story, we have, indeed, moved closer to the world that Bradbury presents. Video games such as "Guitar Hero," for example, allow children (and adults) to play the guitar and be a "rock star" without actually knowing how to play the guitar. Virtually reality games such as "Grand Theft Auto" have, indeed, tapped into the violent nature of humans and have, in fact, been blamed by some for the increase in violence in children.

The characters in the story are shown doing nothing, yet they are always *busy* doing nothing. They are shown "working too hard" (9), "preoccupied" (11) and "being busy" (11), yet they don't actually *do* anything. Lydia even confesses "Maybe I don't have enough to do" (9). Ironically, the parents decide to take a vacation so they can do some work.

Bradbury discloses this cultural code by employing a technique that Genette terms "paralepsis" (*Narrative*

195)—the narrator's presenting of information that the focus character would not know. The narrator of "The Veldt" does this primarily through tone. For example, on page 7 the narrator uses an ironic tone to describe the wonders of the Happy-life home:

> They walked down the hall of their sound-proofed, Happy-life home, which had cost them thirty thousand dollars installed, this house which clothed and fed and rocked them to sleep and played and sang and was good to them.

The narration focuses on the trivial, worthless machines, a technique that highlights the characters' laziness. Obviously the machines do some important work around the house, but the narrator mockingly shows that the characters cannot even tie their own shoes or go to sleep without these mechanical devices.

Throughout the narrative the reader understands more about George's predicament than George does himself. The narrator relates information that George already has but which he fails to see the significance of. The ironic tone makes the reader see this significance, namely, that George and Lydia, like the society they represent, have become enslaved by their technology.

Barthes' last code, the textual code, appears whenever a text speaks of itself, or about writing. Although "The Veldt" has no obvious textual code, the idea of fantasy coming to life could be considered one when examined in the context of the complete collection. The idea of the children's fantasy coming to life recalls the Illustrated Man's tattoos coming to life. The prologue of *The Illustrated Man*, which occurs just before "The Veldt," ends with the line: "The first illustration quivered and came to life..." (5). As the first story in the collection, it is no accident that "The Veldt" foregrounds the theme of the entire work—illusion or fantasy becoming reality.

"The Veldt" illustrates the destructive potential of fantasy. Yes, fantasy can become reality: we can work to make our dreams come true, as the adults of the story did in creating their technology, or we can use our child-like powers of imagination to do so. Dreams, however, are a double-edged sword. The adults become so consumed with their technology that they fail to realize what might result from their creation. The children, likewise, are possessed by their own imaginations. The fantasy, then, when allowed complete liberty, becomes a dangerous, destructive entity. The narrator of *The Illustrated Man* learns of this destructive power by watching the first illustration come to life. As he watches the second "stir to life" (19), he will learn another lesson, that of fantasy's redemptive possibilities.

CHAPTER TWO

"KALEIDOSCOPE": THE REDEMPTIVE FANTASY

The second story in *The Illustrated Man*, "Kaleidoscope," originally appeared in *Thrilling Wonder Stories* in October, 1948. This story is one of Bradbury's few real "space" stories, yet, like most of Bradbury's work, it has its basis more in psychology than in physics or astronomy.

"Kaleidoscope" begins immediately after the explosion of a rocket. The survivors, helpless and doomed to die, communicate through their radios as they fall away from each other across the miles of space. This is not an action story of exploding rockets, but an introspective portrait of the dying Hollis examining his life. Much of the narrative concerns itself with what might have been rather than what actually was. Hollis examines his life in terms of missed possibilities and this conditional, subjunctive viewpoint forms an important part of the narrative.

Unlike "The Veldt", "Kaleidoscope" begins with a summary to fill in the background description of the exploding rocket, an action necessary to understand the predicament of the characters. Only five lines are spent describing the explosion; the disaster is handled quickly and efficiently so that the real story can begin—the mental struggle of a character who knows he is about to die.

Bradbury is faced with a paradox in this story. The characters have several hours to live—a short time to actually "live," yet a very long time to think about dying. The author must, therefore, make this narrative time pass quickly enough to sustain the reader's interest, while making it pass slowly enough to give Hollis time to worry about his situation. Death must be prolonged, yet imminent.

As he does in "The Veldt," Bradbury again employs

a cinematic technique to solve a narrative problem. In an eight page story he uses six ellipses to create ten distinct scenes connected by an indeterminate amount of time. The first ellipsis, on page 20, spans a short but distinct span: "A period of perhaps ten minutes elapsed while the first terror died..." Seventeen lines later, a space between paragraphs marks an indefinite passage of time, as do the next two ellipses on page 21 and 22. These indefinite ellipses fill up periods that would burden a short, introspective work like "Kaleidoscope," and create the proper time sense for free-floating, disoriented characters who would have no concept of the exact movement of the clock.

The last two ellipses prove particularly interesting. An ellipsis occurs on page 25 that covers a mere second of time: "It was a second later that he discovered that his right foot was cut sheer away." This rapid, almost instantaneous passage of a moment in time calls attention to the quickness of nature's destructive forces while offering a contrast between instant death and the prolonged agony of a slow, imminent death. The last ellipsis, on page 27, allows Bradbury to change narrative focus, as we have already seen with the ending of "The Veldt." This allows Hollis' death to occur "offstage," and offers the change of perspective—from Hollis to the child—needed to make the surprise ending effective.

"Kaleidoscope" appears to be a simple enough story upon first reading. Yet the story contains several themes that prove it to be quite complex when examined in detail. I will diagram the story as a grammatical equation to expose some of these themes.

A-S> A opt S> A sks S thru Sp> A-H> Sp des Rk> A opt H> Sp des A> A cre H thru C> F bec R> A+S thru D

Where:

A= adult (Hollis)   -= negation of trait
C= child   >= leads to
F= fantasy   opt= wishes (for)
R= reality   cre= creates
Sp= space   des= destroys

H= happiness bec= becomes
Rk= rocket += gaining of trait
sks= seeks D= death
S= success thru= through

Translating this equation gives the basic story reduced to a chronological sequence. An adult, Hollis, who lacks success yet desires it, seeks success in space. His preoccupation with achievement makes him an unhappy man. When his rocket explodes and he is hurled into space to die, he discovers this unhappiness. His dying wish is to be happy or, since that is now impossible, to at least create happiness. When space actually does destroy him, he does create a moment of happiness when a child sees him as a "falling star" and makes a wish on his behalf. Thus, Hollis' fantasy (to leave a mark on the world, to become successful) becomes reality. Hollis, ironically, achieves success through his own death. In this story, as in "The Veldt," the child's *belief* in wishes coming true makes the fantasy come true.

This equation isolates three major themes that work

together to enrich the meaning of the story. The first theme is that of space, which I will look at in more detail using Barthes' action and connotative codes. The second concerns death, and can be explained in terms of Bartes' cultural, psychoanalytical, textual, and symbolic codes. The third theme, wishes, appears in Barthes' symbolic code as the opposition of fantasy and reality, and in the cultural code of childhood.

The connotative code of "Kaleidoscope" describes space, or the cosmos, as a major "character" in the story. Space is always referred to in titanic, god-like terms, while mortal characters are connoted by smallness. The very first sentence of the story introduces this code: "The first concussion cut the rocket like a giant can opener. The men were thrown into space like a dozen wriggling silverfish." Later they fall like "pebbles", "as jackstones are scattered from a gigantic throw" (20). Space "weaves its strange voices... on a great, dark loom" (20), and Stone refers to the meteor cluster as "they" (26) rather than "it."

Space, in addition to being described in god-like

terms, is also described by its randomness. The image of the kaleidoscope itself implies randomness, and the rocket is destroyed by a chance act, as if some god casually opens a tin can with a giant can opener. The spacemen are scattered in haphazard patterns; the use of the passive verb (The men were thrown.... They were scattered) in the opening paragraph connotes a randomness over which the men have no control. Later, the spacemen are described as "snowflakes" (20), the epitome of randomness. "Kaleidoscope" illustrates the theme of the random universe, of a scientific God who acts through natural selection and quantum physics rather than through moral design.

Since "Kaleidoscope" contains very little action, as such (the explosion of the ship and the death of Hollis both occur offstage), the action code plays a minor role in the story. The action that does occur, however, follows a distinct pattern. A diagram of this would resemble the spokes of a wheel, radiating out from the center of an exploded spacecraft. The microcosmic universe of the spacemen parallels the naturalistic expanding universe as postulated in the "Big Bang" theory, where each galaxy and star speeds away from its neighbors at the speed of light. Each spaceman becomes a tiny star in this microcosm, a "falling star" of sorts.

The second major theme of "Kaleidoscope" is death. The cultural code of the story exposes twentieth century American attitudes towards death. In our culture one must "die like a man." When one of the spacemen breaks this cultural expectation and begins screaming (21), Hollis smashes his faceplate, which kills him instantly. "It was the best way," Hollis rationalizes. And when the men begin to argue among themselves, Applegate reminds them "this is a bad way to die" (25), and they settle their differences according to the dictates of culture.

As we have seen in "The Veldt," Bradbury does not write science fiction in the strict definition of the term. Psychology and sociology play a more important role in his stories than astronomy and physics. "Kaleidoscope," though it may appear to be a story about rockets and space, actually relies on the "science" of psychology for its main premise and to add a realistic dimension to the theme of death.

Looking at the story from a psychological perspective sheds some interesting insights into Bradbury's death themes if we deviate from strict Freudian interpretation and examine the general psychology of dying. Since the narrative describes the thoughts and emotions of men who know they are about to die, we must go beyond the cultural or sociological aspect of dying, and examine the psychology of death.

Elizabeth Kubler-Ross, in her book *On Death and Dying* (1969), postulated that terminally ill patients go through five stages once they learn of their imminent death. Although every individual may not pass through every stage, patients will pass through the sequence in a predictable order. In the first stage, denial, the patient refuses to accept his death. This leads to anger, the second stage. In the third stage, bargaining, the patient tries to "make a deal" with his god, often promising to lead a better life if he is spared. Depression follows, and, finally, the patient enters the last stage, acceptance of his own death.

The dying spacemen in "Kaleidoscope" experience four of the five stages of death. The first stage, denial, occurs on page 21 as Stimpson denies the severity of the situation: "I don't believe this; I don't believe any of this is happening." Another character calls his predicament a "bad dream" (21). The second stage, anger, appears immediately after denial on page 21: "Hollis felt for the first time the impossibility of his position. A great anger filled him..." Anger continues through page 23 as the spacemen argue and try to hurt one another. The third stage, bargaining, is conspicuously absent from this narrative. The absence of God enhances the random universe theme mentioned earlier. Since the characters do not seem to believe in God, at least not in the traditional sense, they have no deity to bargain with. Space itself is the closest thing to God in this story, and space/physics/biology operates by unyielding laws that cannot be changed. These characters know that one cannot negotiate with gravity. The fourth stage, depression, strikes Hollis once he realizes he has no memories: "He felt tears start into his eyes and roll down his face" (24). Acceptance, the final stage, appears on page 26-27 as Hollis finds himself alone with his thoughts.

> I'll burn, he thought, and be scattered in ashes all over the continental lands. I'll be put to use. Just a little bit, but ashes are ashes and they'll add to the land.
> He fell swiftly... objective, objective all of the time now, not sad or happy or anything.... (27).

The story successfully shows the emotional stages that man (or twentieth century American man, at least) passes through when he knows his own death is imminent. This story "predicts" the finding of modern psychology by some twenty years, just as other science fiction writers have "predicted" advances in technology. Bradbury's use of the human sciences for story ideas (even though they may occur in a technological setting) helped to stretch the boundaries of the science fiction genre to accommodate the "new wave" stories of today.

We can examine the theme of death from another perspective by using Barthes' symbolic code, which hinges upon the binary oppositions of silence and speech, or between communication and non-communication. To communicate means to live. Non-communication implies death. As long as their voices can be heard, the men have hope since they have life. As the voices fade and drift further away, hope fades and death draws near.

This symbolic code, in a sense, resembles a textual code since it equates narrative (or storytelling) with life—a common enough theme in literature (In *One Thousand and One Nights*, for example, Scheherazade lives as long as she can narrate tales) and recalls the prologue/epilogue framework of the collection as a whole, where the narrator escapes death and lives to tell the stories that compose *The Illustrated Man*. "Kaleidoscope" equates narrative with life and silence with death. Hollis reflects upon the meaning of life and finds that it resembles a film, a picture narrative: "When life is over it is like the flicker of a bright film, an instant on the screen...." (23). Silence, the lack of narrative, is described in fearful terms, as a "terrible silence" (22). When one man's screaming threatens to disrupt communication between the men, Hollis destroys him because he was "making it impossible for them to talk to one another" (21). The men instinctively need this communication, this narrative, to prolong their lives. The voices appear as living entities as they "vibrate" (26), and the network of voices becomes a "great loose brain" (26). And when the men move too far away from one another to communicate, their voices do not merely drift out of radio range, but actually die: "Their voices had died like echoes of the words of God spoken..." (26).

From a structuralist point of view, antithesis forms an important part of a narrative; as we have already seen, binary oppositions determine meaning within a text. Barthes' symbolic code can be used to call attention to the oppositions within a story and show how these oppositions produce meaning. The textual code links the oppositions of speech/silence with life/death to produce meaning, and, by so doing, could be considered a symbolic code as well as a textual one.

Linked to this symbolism of speech/silence, life/death is another antithesis: wishes/memories. The wishes resemble the silence; they represent the narrative that might have been, while memories represent the narrative of what has actually happened. Although Hollis cannot see the difference between wishes and memories at first, he soon distinguishes between the two. Lespere will "live" even in death because he has no memories, and will be remembered by others. Hollis, with no memories of his own, and no one to remember him, will die. At the very end of the narrative, Hollis achieves narrative "life" of his own, at least in a small way. Although he is burned up in the earth's atmosphere, he is given narrative life by a small boy who sees him and speaks: "Look, Mom, look! A falling star!" (27). Hollis' empty life becomes complete through the narrative of the boy and his mother, a narrative which, interestingly enough, takes the form of a wish that may come true and become a pleasant memory. Hollis will be remembered by the boy; Hollis' wish to do something good becomes a reality through another wish—the boy's. Thus, in "Kaleidoscope," as in "The Veldt," fantasy becomes reality because of a child.

This fantasy/reality theme returns us to Barthes' cultural code once again. In contemporary Western culture, children are taught that their wishes may come true, if they believe hard enough. This cultural theme has given rise to such myths as Santa Claus, the Tooth Fairy, and, of course, wishing upon a star. One would not expect such myths to inhabit the space-age world of "Kaleidoscope," and, for the most part, they do not. Yet, within the realm of childhood, anything becomes possible. Modern society allows, even encourages children to believe in such things; an adult with such beliefs would be considered immature or abnormal. Yet the children of Bradbury's stories can make their wishes come true simply by believing hard enough.

For them, the myth is entirely real.

"Kaleidoscope" teaches the narrator his second lesson about fantasy and reality. In "The Veldt" he has learned about the destructive potential of making our wishes come true. In this story he learns, once again, that fantasy can come to life; yet this lesson shows how this transformation may be redemptive instead of destructive. In "Kaleidoscope" the adult's wish becomes real with the help of a child's imagination. This transformation involves cooperation between the adult and the child. This cooperation, this combination of adult knowledge with child-like innocence, produces a fantasy that gives life to the adult and hope to the child.

Lest our narrator become too optimistic, however, he must learn the lesson of the delusional fantasy, which will appear in our next story.

CHAPTER THREE
"THE LONG RAIN": THE SELF-DELUSIONAL FANTASY

"The Long Rain", the sixth story in the collection, is set on Venus, a planet with perpetual rain. The premise of the story is simple: a rocket crashes in the rainforest and the four survivors must make their way to one of the Sun Domes, outposts that have been built on the planet for the human colonists. The story was first published in *Planet Stories* in 1950, when little was known about Venus—its surface was not mapped in detail until the Project Magellan mission in 1990-91. "The Long Rain" was included in the film adaptation of *The Illustrated Man*, and was later adapted into film for Ray Bradbury Theater in 1992. We have already seen a rocket crash in Kaleidoscope, and the father in

"Rocket Man" (which follows "The Long Rain") is also killed in a space accident.

As we have seen, many of Bradbury's stories use a cinematic technique with ellipses to jump from one scene to the other so as to speed up the action. In this story, however, the narrative must be slowed down in order to create a sense of monotony caused by the rain, and yet, the reader's interest must be kept alive. Bradbury accomplishes this by spicing together scenes and descriptive pauses that employ interesting, poetic language.

The story begins with a description of the rain, "...a hard rain, a perpetual rain, a sweating and steaming rain," (53) evoking images of Noah and the great flood. This descriptive pause forces the reader to experience the rain through all of the senses as it "shaved the grass" and "shrank" the skin. The description allows the reader time to recall and relive the worst rainstorms that they have ever experienced before they are dropped into narrative time. The description is eloquent and interesting, even as it holds the actual narrative back and slows down time.

The description is then interrupted by dialogue that introduces the first scene and central question: "How much further?" The dialogue introduces the characters and then another descriptive pause brings in images of whiteness caused by the rain. Dialogue poses additional questions and descriptions, and between the two narrative techniques the reader is both pulled along and held back at the same time. The effect, indeed, conveys a sense of monotony, a black and white world of endless rain that never changes, and yet scenes introduce conflicts one after another: the return to the rocket as they find they have travelled in a circle; and the madness and destruction of three of the survivors, one by one. Bradbury is able to prolong the agony of the main character while still keeping the reader interested in the tale.

Analepses, or flashbacks, occur rarely in this story, as most of it occurs in the present with the men trudging through the endless rain. The back-story is revealed in occasional sentences within the description: "...far back behind them somewhere, a rocket in which they had fallen..." (54), and through dialogue, as when Packard recalls the torture he once suffered from a bully when he was a boy (60). Background information about the Venusians, the Sun Domes and a history of men "going crazy" from the rain is relayed in dialogue as well.

Prolepses, narrative devices that foreshadow future narrative events, occur more frequently in the story and may play a role in helping the reader to decipher the ending, which can be read two different ways. At first reading, it seems as though the lieutenant finds the Sun Dome at the story's conclusion, "warm, hot, yellow, and very fine" (65). After a more careful reading, however, the story becomes ambiguous, as we revisit the madness that the rain brought to the rest of the crew, madness that caused one of them to try to drown himself, and cause the other to shoot him and then later shoot himself. One might wonder if the lieutenant really does find the dome, or if he is delusional.

The first indication of this ambiguity appears almost immediately in the first scene of dialogue, when the lieutenant is asked how much further, and he responds "Another hour or two from here" (53).

> "Are you lying to keep us happy?" the man asks.
> "I'm lying to keep you happy. Shut up!" the lieutenant responds.

While this might appear to be an off-the-cuff remark, the lying theme reappears just a few paragraphs later, in the same scene, when the lieutenant is again accused of lying to raise the men's hopes.

> "No, now I'm lying to myself. This is one of those times when you've got to lie. I can't take much more of this" (54).

Throughout the journey, the lieutenant continues to delude himself and his men into thinking they are within reach of the Sun Dome.

> "Another hour" he says again. (63)

This ability to lie to himself shows that the protagonist is capable of self-delusion and false optimism. In this story, even the compass, normally a symbol of consistency, lies and gives false readings. So is the Sun Dome at the end just another delusion? Is the cot really a sanctuary where "one might lie, exposed and bare, to drink in the... bright light..." (65) or is it his grave where he has fallen and is drinking in the rain?

> "He slipped and fell. Lie here, he thought; it's the wrong one. Lie here.... Drink all you want" (64).

According to Bradbury's narrator, self-delusion is a natural trait of humankind: "They couldn't believe that there wasn't some way to help the man. It was the natural act of men who have not accepted death until they have touched it...." (57).

The foreshadowing devices show the process of how the men are driven insane by the incessant rain. The psychoanalytical code of Barthes also shows the deterioration of the men. The "science" of the story is obviously flawed now that we know that Venus is not an ocean planet. But Bradbury's stories are experiments in the social sciences, and psychology, as we have seen in "Kaleidoscope." In this case, Bradbury deposits his characters into an environment of endless rain, which could exist on any planet, and we watch to see what happens.

The first man, who remains unnamed in the story, jumps up in the middle of the lightning storm and is killed, leaving Simmons, Pickard, and the lieutenant. Pickard related the story of how he was tormented by a bully and "must have gone a little mad" (60). Pickard succumbs next, first firing his gun at the rain, and then giving up, standing with his head up so he can breathe water and drown.

"He can't even feel you," Simmons says before he shoots Pickard. Then he justifies his actions: "You saw his face. Insane" (63) And the lieutenant agrees with him.

Simmons survives the night, but by morning he, too gives in. First he loses his hearing. "My ears. They've gone out on me" (63).

Recognizing that he, too, is on the brink, he decides to take his own life.

> "I'm not crazy yet, but I'm the next thing to it. I don't want to go out that way... I'm going to use this gun on myself" (63).

The lieutenant, the most hopeful of the men, lasts the longest. But his hearing is gone, too: "The lieutenant didn't even hear the sound of the gun" (64).

A few lines later, he, too, considers suicide: "Another five minutes and then I'll walk into the sea and keep walking."

References are constantly made to the rain driving people mad. Venus is compared to Chinese water torture, but on a "big scale" where "you go crazy from just being soggy" (54).

While the psychoanalytical code show the deterioration of the men's minds, the connotative code shows the decay of their bodies. All color has been washed from the men, their faces have turned pale, their eyes were white, and their hair was white. Their uniforms were turning white and green with fungus.

> "Venus bleached everything away in a few months" (55).

The dead crewmates are completely taken over by the planet, which foreshadows what will happen to the living men should they fail.

> "Green fungus was growing up out of the mouths of the two dead men" (56).

The survivors are unable to sleep, and suffer from headaches, and are blinded and deafened by the rain.

Interestingly enough, when the lieutenant finds the Sun Dome, he has already lost his hearing—he could not hear the shot from Simmons' gun—and his hands have gone numb. His vision conveys most of the images of the dome.

> "He stood for a moment looking about" (64).

Here he sees everything he had hoped for, even the steaming cup of hot chocolate the men had fantasized about earlier.

The connotative code introduces more ambiguity, however:

> "He put his hands to his eyes. He saw other men moving towards him, but said nothing to them. He waited and opened his eyes, and looked...." (65).

The immediate question is how he could have seen men moving towards him if he had his eyes closed. Couple this with the previous paragraph with "a phonograph from which music was playing quietly", which is contradicted by the fact that he has gone deaf and, as the story later says, "there was no sound in the room," and this leads us to conclude that the lieutenant must be hallucinating. The Sun Dome seems too good to be true. It probably was.

The symbolic code contrasts the sun and light with the rain and clouds. The sun, as symbolized by the

Sun Dome, gives life and hope. Indeed, psychologists have identified "seasonal depression syndrome" in people who do not get enough sunlight, and statistics show higher suicide rates in countries that have long, dark winters. It is only natural, then, that the lieutenant would envision the light of the Sun Dome in his fantasy. In fact, when the men are thinking about the dome, they fantasize as a group, and Bradbury uses the pronoun "They" to describe it: "... they thought of the Sun Dome, somewhere ahead of them, shining in the jungle rain" (55). This group fantasy perfectly matches the vision that the lieutenant sees at the end, even to the detail of the hot chocolate with the marshmallow.

Water, of course, is also a life-giving element; however, in this story, too much of a good thing becomes destructive. A viable planet would need a balance of sun and water. Too much of either would make it an uninhabitable world.

"We're not made for water," one of the men says.

The plot of "The Long Rain" is more difficult to diagram, but, like the other stories we have examined, it involves the search for happiness, in this case symbolized by the Sun Dome. Assuming that the lieutenant has, indeed, fantasized the dome, we have the following diagram:

A-H> A opt H> A cre H thru F> A+H (D thru F)

where:

A= adult	opt=wishes	cre=creates
F= fantasy	-=negation of trait	+=gains
H=happiness	>=leads to	thru= through
D= death		

The diagram shows the lieutenant as an unhappy adult at the story's outset as he is stranded on Venus and wishes for happiness and safety in the form of the Sun Dome. Ultimately, he creates this happiness (the Sun Dome) through a fantasy that results in his death. In "Kaleidoscope", Hollis' death causes a fantasy to be created; in "The Long Rain" this idea is reversed and the creation of a fantasy results in death. Unlike the destructive fantasy of "The Veldt", however, this death is a kinder one as the lieutenant dies happily by lying to himself.

"The Long Rain" is a successful story because it explores the code of ambiguity that is first introduced by the hermeneutic code early on in the story—who, if anyone, will survive? The men die off in a predictable order: the cynic goes first, followed by Pickard, who has a history of going "a little mad." Simmons holds out a little longer, but the lieutenant, the most optimistic and the leader because of his rank, finds the Sun Dome in the end, even if it is only in his delusion. The story is ambiguous about whether or not the lieutenant is really "saved," though the fact that he sees men coming towards him with his eyes closed, and hears soft music in a silent room imply that the Sun Dome is, in fact, a delusion, a "lie to himself" that he has created as he faces a death that he cannot accept.

Placed in the context of *The Illustrated Man* as a whole, this story illustrates a different kind of fantasy.

It is not destructive, as is the fantasy of "The Veldt" and is not redemptive, as in "Kaleidoscope." It is a delusion, but it is a positive one, similar in some ways to the fantasy coming true in "Kaleidoscope", only in this case the lieutenant is lying to himself, and his death causes no benefit to anyone. The delusion cannot save his life, but can ease his death as we picture him slowly drowning in the rain, while believing he is drinking in the light of the Sun Dome. We can, then, deceive ourselves to the point where we believe our own delusions, even if they are not real. The fantasy becomes reality in his mind at least. In the case of the lieutenant, that is not such a bad thing, since it seems that he is doomed anyway. But as we will see in the next story, the narrator must be aware of his surroundings and of reality to prevent fantasy from becoming a destructive force again, as it did in "The Veldt."

CHAPTER FOUR

"ZERO HOUR": THE DESTRUCTIVE FANTASY REVISITED

The fourth story in my analysis, "Zero Hour," is the next to the last tale in *The Illustrated Man* and bears a strong thematic resemblance to "The Veldt." It is, in fact, an emphatic restatement of the destructive fantasy that we examined in that first story. As the narrator nears the close of *The Illustrated Man*, it becomes necessary for him to experience the destructive fantasy once again, and for him to restate this important lesson in his own narrative.

"Zero Hour" tells the tale of a group of children playing a fantasy game they call "invasion." The fantasy of the game comes to life at the end of the tale, as we learn that the game is, in fact, a real invasion by hostile creatures from another planet who have used the children to slip past the earth's defenses.

The title of the story, "Zero Hour," immediately poses an enigma that will not be resolved until the story's end. "Zero Hour" creates a sense of something important happening at a certain time; as a military code signifying the time of an invasion, it conjures images of action on a grand scale. Bradbury poses the problem—just what will happen at zero hour? The answer, of course, is delayed until the last page of the story as Bradbury carefully ticks away time until the enigma's resolution.

As the title itself indicates, time plays an important role in "Zero Hour." The title refers to the moment of the invasion and the children continually worry about a "five o'clock deadline" (174). On page 172, Mink speaks of four "dimens-shuns" so we can deduce that Drill will invade through the fourth dimension, which, of course, is time in Einstein's universe.

Since time is so important to this story, the speed of movement takes on special importance. The entire story is structured around time and the movement of the narrative toward five o'clock, or "zero hour." Thus, time becomes a countdown, of sorts, a structure of the discourse, and Bradbury makes periodic mention of this countdown to help keep the reader posted as to how much time remains until zero hour.

Seven scenes compose the story, separated by a combination of summary and ellipsis. Base time begins in the morning (169), moves through lunch (171), and counts down to five o'clock (175). Bradbury uses four ellipses to move the narrative forward in quick bursts while keeping the reader informed of the hour of the day. The first ellipsis moves from morning to lunch time: "At lunch Mink gulped her milk at one toss and was at the door" (17). Bradbury devotes the next two pages to dialogue between Mink and her mother as she eats lunch, then makes a chronological leap to four o'clock and the next ellipsis:

> "Thanks for lunch!" Mink ran out, then stuck her head back in. "Mom, I'll be sure you won't be hurt much, really!"

"Well thanks," said Mom.

Slam went the door.

At four o'clock the audio-visor buzzed. (173)

Bradbury uses time to speed the narrative in the beginning of the story by quickly moving the reader through the hours as he counts down to zero hour. Yet, as zero hour draws near, the author structures time for a different purpose—to slow down the narrative and build suspense. Whereas only four and a half pages are used to move from morning to four o'clock, almost two pages are devoted to a single hour from four o'clock to zero hour, beginning with a long scene of dialogue between Mrs. Morris and Helen on the audio-visor (173-74), followed by a dialogue between Mrs. Morris and Mink (174-75), and a descriptive pause showing Mrs. Morris relaxing, "sipping a little beer from a half-empty glass" (175). Bradbury uses two ellipses to move through this last hour, yet these ellipses seem to slow time down rather than speed it up. The first one, on page 174, is an indefinite ellipsis, a white space between paragraphs. It is followed by a summary, "The hour drowsed by," which slows time to a crawl. On the following page an ellipsis states that "time passed" (175). Finally, the singing of a clock makes the reader aware that zero hour has arrived: "Five o'clock—five o'clock. Time's a-wasting. Five o'clock" (175). Two words compose the next paragraph—"Zero Hour," (175) a short, cryptic reminder that the time we have been counting down to has arrived. The brevity of this paragraph alone calls attention to itself as a moment of importance.

The themes of "Zero Hour" restate the lessons of "The Veldt" and may be isolated in the following diagram:

C-P> C opt P> C pl F> A-bel F> F bec R (F des A> C+P

Where:

C= children   pl=play   +=positive trait

A= adult   bel=believe   >= leads to

F= fantasy   bec=become   ( )=occurs offstage
P= power   -= negative trait   des= destroys
opt=wish for

The nouns "fantasy" and "reality" and the verbs "create" and "destroy" thematize both "Zero Hour" and "The Veldt." In this story the game represents the fantasy or wish of the children, just as Africa does in "The Veldt." The children in both stories create a fantasy that becomes real and destroys their parents as a result of a power struggle between them. The children in "Zero Hour" may seem more innocent than Wendy and Peter since an outside force tricks them into causing destruction, but they are motivated by power, nonetheless. If the aliens conquer the earth, the children are promised privileges: "No more baths. And we can stay up till ten o'clock and go to two televisor shows...." (173). They will also be given power: "They're going to let us run the world.... I might be queen" (173).

Using Barthes' semiotic codes, we can elaborate on these themes further. The connotative code can be used to develop the opposition between children and adults, the cultural code can be used to examine society's views on imagination, and the symbolic code can be used to demonstrate how these cultural forces relate to the psychology of the imagination.

Every phase of the adult world is portrayed with connotations of inactivity, connotations that show them as being lazy, complacent, and vulnerable to destruction. The business world does not resemble the hectic activity of Wall Street, but resembles the quietness of a library: "businessmen in their quiet offices taping their voices or watching televisors" (170). The rockets in this society do not blast off or even travel; instead they "hovered like darning needles in the blue sky" (170). In the descriptive pause at the bottom of page 170, a series of linking verbs and passive verbs reinforce the sense of inactivity:

> There was the universal, quiet conceit and easiness of men accustomed to peace, quite certain there would never be trouble again. Arm in arm, men all over the earth were a united front. The perfect weapons were held in

equal trust by all nations. A situation of incredibly beautiful balance had been brought about.

There were no traitors among men (170).

Even when active verbs are used, they show inaction: "hummed", "hovered", "illuminated", and "drowsed."

This connotative code restates an earlier theme from "The Veldt," and warns of the dangers of too much technology. In this society, also, machines do the work that people would normally do. In fact, just about the only work there is to do, it seems, is fix the machines: "Repairmen came to repair the vacuum elevators in houses, to fix fluttering television sets or hammer upon stubborn delivery tubes" (169). Mrs. Morris, like the mother in "The Veldt," has little to do. At lunch she prepares the meal by pressing a button (171); all she had to do was open a can. When she talks with her friend in Scranton, however, both parents say they are tired (173), explaining their fatigue with the excuse: "children underfoot" (173). As the reader can plainly see, the children are not underfoot, but are outside playing by themselves while Mrs. Morris sits in the electric chair that massages her back.

The inactivity of the adults leads to a complacency that leads to their downfall. Because they have become lazy instead of wary, they make easy targets to an invader who has energy, action, and motivation.

The children, on the other hand, are always shown as active. In the very first paragraph they are moving, "catapulting", "Flying", "climbing", "laughing", "tumbling", and "screaming" (169). Everything they do is charged with energy. Even as Mink eats lunch, her mother tells her to "slow down." This motion forms a dramatic contrast to the slow-moving adults who are always tired and "jealous of the fierce energy of the wild tots" (170). The transition from child to adult is a gradual one, of course, and as the children grow older their energy level decreases. The older children, for example, enjoy hiking instead of running and "play a more dignified version of hide-and-seek on their own" (169).

The cultural code focuses primarily on the cultural expectations of children and adults. It is acceptable for young children to use their imaginations and to pretend; however, once the child reaches the age of ten or so, he is discouraged from playing childish games that involve imagining and pretending. Older children make fun of those who play these creative games, and adults carry this to the extreme of concentrating exclusively on reality. In the adult world, imagination is only accepted in such creative (and often misunderstood) individuals as artists, writers, and musicians.

The children in "Zero Hour" are quite conscious of this cultural expectation. When Joe, a twelve-year-old boy, wants to play the invasion game, Mink tells him "You're old" (170). Later she explains: "We're having trouble with guys like Pete Britz and Dale Jerrick. They're growing up. They make fun. They're worse than parents. They won't believe in Drill" (173).

We can use Barthes' symbolic code to accent the theme of fantasy and reality that is so important to *The Illustrated Man*. The children live in a world of creativity and imagination, a world where fantasy can become a reality. The adults lack energy, lack imagination, and lack the creativity to bring fantasy to life. The children and the adults symbolize the two sides of human nature—the creative side, and the rational, logical side. The children symbolize the artistic nature of mankind, the writers, artists, poets, and musicians. The adults represent the analytical side of human nature, the mathematicians, scientists, and inventors.

In "Zero Hour," the children have the capacity to create and imagine, to be artistic. This almost magical ability is necessary to bring fantasy to life, as any artist will testify. Yet this creative ability needs organization and understanding of the adult in order to function properly. A child might be a "natural poet" (Rico, 74), but without the knowledge of poetic technique this natural talent will amount to nothing. In fact, Bradbury shows that the imagination, when allowed to "run wild" without any adult interference, can become a destructive force. The "impressionable" children can imagine beings from another dimension, from another universe, and make them a real part of *this* universe without thinking of the consequences. On the other hand, using logic exclusively can be equally destructive—the logical, rational world of the adults is destroyed because they cannot imagine "impossible" possibilities such as an invasion through the fourth dimension.

The narrator of *The Illustrated Man* has learned this lesson in "The Veldt," but he must now be reminded of it once again before he watches the last illustration come to life. In this last illustration he will assemble all of the lessons he has learned and discover the artistic secret he will need to become a storyteller and narrate the tales in this collection.

CHAPTER FIVE

"THE ROCKET": THE ARTISTIC FANTASY

"The Rocket," first published in 1950, is the most optimistic tale in the *The Illustrated Man* and its place as the last story in the collection is no accident. The story relies more on character than any other of the previous tales in this analysis, and does not require a surprise ending for its effect.

"The Rocket" is set in the future when rockets are as common as airplanes are today. A poor man named Bodoni dreams of travelling to Mars on a rocket; he saves all of his money for a "rainy day," though the thought of using the money for a Mars trip is always on his mind. Once he has saved all of his extra money for the trip, however, he realizes he does not have enough money for his family to come with him. The dream can come true, but only at the cost of his family's happiness. Instead of purchasing the ticket for the Mars trip, he buys a useless rocket that has been junked. He fixes the junk rocket in such a way that when his children climb on board they believe they are actually going to Mars. Bodoni perpetuates the charade, and his children experience the dream of going to Mars, while he accepts the fantasy trip as being as good as the real thing. His wife, who refused to climb into the junk rocket, realizes that her husband has created a magical fantasy for the children; at the end of the story she, too, asks to take the make-believe trip.

As in all the stories analyzed so far, the actual story begins long before the first sentence of the discourse. Bradbury effectively condenses a long story into a single, concise period of time in which a crisis occurs. As we have seen in the previous stories, this technique allows the author to begin the conflict immediately and keep the reader's interest.

Although "The Rocket" occurs almost exclusively

in base time, it begins as the culmination of events that have taken place over the course of twenty years of Bodoni's life. The actual story begins twenty years before base time when he opens his junkyard, a decision that dooms him to a life of poverty and puts an effective end to his dream of travelling to Mars. With his marriage and the births of his children, this dream slips further and further away.

The story opens with a crisis; Bodoni has saved money for new machinery that he desperately needs, but the amount of cash is sufficient for one person to travel on the rocket. He confronts a decision—should he buy the machinery, or go to Mars? And if he chooses the Mars trip, which member of his family should go?

When the narrative begins, Bodoni has not made up his mind. We find him gazing up at the stars thinking about his fantasy. When his friend, Bramante, appears, a dialogue begins that efficiently fills in the background that has led to this crisis and results in Bodoni's decision:

> Bodoni hesitated. "Old man, I've saved three thousand dollars. It took me six years to save it. For my business, to invest in machinery. But every night for a month now, I've been awake. I hear the rockets. I think. And tonight I've made up my mind. One of us will fly to Mars!" His eyes were shining and dark (178).

This brief bit of dialogue efficiently fills in the background of two past time frames—the six years Bodoni has saved his money, and the month he has been thinking about the rocket—and also directly states Bodoni's decision. The dialogue immediately following this section states the major conflict for the remainder of the story:

> "...How will you choose? Who will go? If you go, your wife will hate you.... When you tell your amazing trip to her, over the years, won't bitterness gnaw at her?
>
> "No, no!"

"Yes! And your children? Will their lives be filled with the memory of Papa, who flew to Mars while they stayed here?" (178)

Once Bradbury starts the conflict moving, he uses the cinematic technique we have seen in each of the previous stories to move the plot rapidly toward its conclusion. Altogether, the eight page story contains eight scenes; seven ellipses cut from one scene to the next like the lens of a camera.

The first scene opens with a one paragraph summary of Bodoni's sleepless nights, then begins the dialogue with Bramante. This scene, as I have shown, fills in important background information and gives us Bodoni's decision, which will create conflict throughout the remainder of the story. An ellipsis on page 179 transports the reader into the next scene, breakfast, which shows the family deciding that no one will take the trip to Mars after all. An ellipsis on page 180 moves base time forward in the day and shows Bodoni at work in his junkyard. This scene introduces the junk rocket into the story. An ellipsis on page 181 moves base time ahead to that night, and the delivery of the junk rocket. In this scene Bodoni conceives his idea for the fantasy trip to Mars. The next scene begins on page 182, following another ellipsis. The short scene intensifies conflict between Bodoni and his wife over the rocket. The seventh scene, following an ellipsis on page 183, describes the fantasy trip to Mars. Finally, the last scene on page 185 shows Bodoni's wife accepting the idea of the fantasy trip to Mars.

Each scene in this story accomplishes a specific task in moving the plot toward its conclusion, without wasting space on unnecessary digressions. Bradbury gives us only the information we need to know, then, once the scene has served its purpose, he cuts away to the next. The action is well-planned and methodical as the plot moves forward one step at a time.

Although "The Rocket" appears to be a simple story, at least in terms of plot, it does explore several complex themes. A plot diagram will help define this:

A-H> A opt F> [A+F> Fm-H]> A-F> A+Rk> A cre F thru Rk> F bec R> Fm+F> A+F> A+H where:

A= adult   opt= wishes   [ ] = possibility
F= fantasy -= negation of trait += gains
H= happiness >=leads to   cre= creates
Rk= rocket thru= thru   bec= becomes
Fm= family R= reality

The equation shows the protagonist lacking happiness in the beginning of the story, but gaining it in the end. Since he needs money to achieve this goal, the theme of money becomes important and will form a cultural code in the story. The rocket, an important noun in the plot, introduces another theme, that of space travel, exploration, and the pioneer spirit. This theme can be seen in terms of Barthes' cultural and connotative codes. Finally, through the verbs "creates", "becomes", and "wishes", and the nouns "fantasy" and "reality," the theme of fantasy becoming reality re-emerges, only in a more optimistic manner than in the previous stories—through artistic creation.

The theme of money can best be examined through

Barthes' cultural code. Although "The Rocket" occurs in the future in a technologically sophisticated society, Bodoni's world is still a capitalistic one. This wonderful technology of the future is available only to those who can afford to buy it. The characters of "The Veldt" and "Zero Hour" depict such wealthy individuals; the characters in "The Rocket," however, lack the money to benefit from the new inventions of the future. Bramante states this idea directly:

> This is a rich man's world.... When I was young they wrote it in fiery letters: THE WORLD OF THE FUTURE! Science, Comfort, and New Things for All! Ha! Eighty years. The future becomes Now! Do we fly rockets? No! We live in shacks like our ancestors before us (178).

According to this story, rich men and poor men will always exist, despite the new advantages of technology. Only those with money will benefit by the new technology: the poor, as always, will be left to desire the things they cannot have, just as Bodoni desires a rocket trip that he cannot afford.

"The Rocket," then, is a study of poverty and hardship and how man adapts to not being able to have the things he wants. The wealthy children in Bradbury's stories ("The Veldt", for example) need complicated technological toys to play with. Yet the children of poor parents who cannot afford these toys play with whatever they can find. Bodoni's three boys fight over a single toy rocket while his daughters play with alien dolls (179), toys that, despite their alien-ness, resemble the toys of today. These children have no three-dimensional nursery to imagine for them, but must use their own imagination to create their fantasies. Having learned how to create and imagine, they can easily believe their father's crude fantasy trip to Mars; the children of "The Veldt" would not have been impressed with Bodini's attempt to create something that their nursery could have created in more realistic detail.

In every culture, parents want more for their children

than they had for themselves. This theme is apparent in "The Rocket"; Bodoni knows he can never travel to Mars, yet he hopes his children will be able to do so. This idea reflects the twentieth century notion that, through hard work, the second generation will achieve more success than the first. Bodoni exemplifies this Puritan work ethic, the foundation of American capitalism: work hard, save your money, and you and your children will gain success.

"The Rocket," though, shows the American dream gone sour. Bodoni has worked hard and saved, but as soon as he "gets ahead," something goes wrong. He saves his money for six long years, only to have his machinery break down and need replacement. This theme shows the reality behind the fantasy of the American Dream. As Bradbury warns, hard work and diligence do not always mean success.

Rocket ships and trips to Mars introduce the second major theme of the story—the age-old fascination of mankind with exploration. The pioneer spirit has burned with exceptional brightness in the American soul, and now that the frontier has vanished, the explorers have turned their attentions to the stars. Bradbury has, of course, developed this idea in many of his works, the most notable, perhaps, being *The Martian Chronicles*, where earthmen colonize Mars much as the early Europeans colonized America.

Many science fiction writers have treated the stars as the exclusive domain of the scientist. Bradbury, however, sees this pioneer spirit in all mankind, scientist and junkman alike. Bodoni, even in his simplicity and poverty, aspires to the stars:

> Many nights Fiorello Bodoni would awaken to hear the rockets sighing in the dark sky. He would tiptoe from bed, certain that his kind wife was dreaming, to let himself out into the night air. For a few moments he would be free of the smells of the old food in the small house by the river. For a silent moment he would let his heart soar alone into space, following the rockets. (177)

Being curious about the stars seems to be a trait common to all men. Even Bramante, the eternal skeptic and realist, admits, "I prefer the rockets myself." (178)

The connotations of the story illustrate mankind's fascination with space by contrasting the ugliness of Bodoni's home with the beauty of the rockets and the stars. Bradbury portrays space and its byproducts in poetic terms: he describes the rockets as "fire fountains" (178) and personifies them as living creatures "sighing" (177) and "murmuring" (178). Even the backup mockup rocket, a piece of scrap metal, in reality, takes on connotations of grandeur with its silver and blue colors of speed and fantasy: "It held the whiteness of the moon and the blueness of the stars" (181). Although the scrap rocket had never left earth, it still "smelled of time and distance" (181).

Space itself takes on even greater connotations as Bradbury describes it in almost religious terms. Bramante tells his friend he will think his wife "holy" (178) if she travels in the rocket. Space, normally thought of as being black, is portrayed as a rainbow of colors. The rocket "dropped pink petals of fire" (184) while "meteors broke into fireworks" (184) and "Red Mars floated near the rocket" (185). Even the alien dolls of the children duplicate the colors of space, "green mannequins with three yellow eyes" (179).

Bodoni's own existence, however, is painted with the ugly connotations and dull colors of a junkyard world that melts down broken dreams. Bodoni's introduction shows him standing half-naked in the darkness, in awe of the rockets above him (177). His friend Bramante sits on a milk crate (178), in contrast to the heavenly scene above him. Every aspect of Bodoni's life is filled with ugliness and mundaneness. His "mountainous wife" (179) lacks physical beauty, and his children are described as "nervous children" (179) with "large noses" (180), not intelligent and not even terribly interesting. Bodoni eats a common breakfast of bacon, eggs, and toast that "curdled within him" (180), and his house contains ordinary, unexciting objects such as brooms and a "silver box" (179) that makes toast (the toaster, a product of technology, is the only object described by bright colors). The children, in an attempt to live in the fantasy world of space, play with toy rockets and alien dolls, but even these exotic toys cannot make Bodoni's home exciting.

The junkyard contains the dullness of metal, and rusted metal at that: "Rusted, unchanged, there stood the padlocked junk yard gate...." (184), and we see it again at night, bathed in darkness and lit by the moon. Bodoni's house is lit with a yellow light, comfortable and warm, but not very exciting.

The contrast between Bodoni's real world and the dream world of his space fantasy reveals Barthes' symbolic code, the bipolar opposition between fantasy and reality. Bodoni represents the dreamer who is chained to the real world, and his junkyard symbolizes this reality where the junk, the broken dreams of the world, comes to be salvaged. Bodoni's "terrible" (182) wrecking machine destroys what is left of the world's broken dreams and puts them out of their miseries. Bramante even advises Bodoni to destroy his own dream: "... buy a new wrecking machine... and pull your dreams apart with it, and smash them to pieces" (178).

Ironically enough, a river runs past this junkyard. This river represents another dream gone bad; the river, a beautiful handiwork of nature, borders a junkyard, the ultimate depiction of ugliness, where it has no doubt become polluted and rusted like Bodoni's junk. Man has destroyed the beauty of the earth, it seems, and must turn to the stars to salvage his dreams.

The Mars rocket symbolizes man's fantasy of reaching the stars. The junkyard opposes this dream by keeping Bodoni chained to the earth and unable to achieve his goals. Yet, as we have seen in the previous stories, fantasy can be turned into reality—dreams can come true, despite impossible odds. Bodoni never abandons his dreams and, ultimately, transforms them into reality with his own hands as he "works fiery magic" (183) upon the scrap rocket. Even though the fantasy can never be entirely real for him, he does, in effect, play Santa Claus and makes the fantasy become real for his children. The children, still having the power of imagination, believe the fantasy and complete the transformation into reality, while the wife, an adult, dismisses the idea as madness. Only at the end of the story, when she sees the magic Bodoni has created for their children, is she prepared also to accept the fantasy.

Unlike the previous stories we have examined, "The Rocket" depicts fantasy becoming reality in a positive manner. "The Veldt" and "Zero Hour" showed the destructive power of fantasy; "Kaleidoscope" showed the redemptive power of fantasy, yet a life was destroyed to bring this redemption about. "The Long Rain" shows a delusional fantasy that leads to death. In this story, however, fantasy becomes real in a beneficial way, and Bodoni is not deluding himself: his "lies" are a conscious artistic creation. An adult is the creative influence that makes the transformation from fantasy to reality, with some help from the children.

Bodoni, the adult, demonstrates that the power to make dreams come true lies within every man, if he has the willpower and imagination to make it happen. His child-like belief in a better life serves as the catalyst that enables him to give his children their fantasy. To the children, the trip to Mars is the real thing. The fantasy trip symbolizes the belief that dreams can come true; Bodoni feels that his children must learn this lesson if they are to survive in the real world of poverty and dejection. Bodoni, by giving his children this dream, encourages them to use their imaginations and to reach for the stars, to quote the cliché. "You're the best father in all the world" (185), his wife says, after she realizes and understands the gift of imagination he has given to them.

We have seen in previous stories that the transformation from fantasy to reality can be destructive if not tempered by maturity of understanding and will. The fantasy of the child can run completely out of control, as we have seen in "The Veldt" and "Zero Hour." The adult, however, can dream constructively if he retains some of the innocence, creativity, and imagination of his childhood. The artistic fantasy results from this combination of child and adult; this theme, which has been hinted at throughout *The Illustrated Man*, culminates in "The Rocket."

Bodoni uses his creative talents coupled with his maturity to create his fantasy rocket trip, an artistic effort of imagination that becomes a masterpiece to his children. He personifies the artist within all mankind; from the desperation of the junkyard he creates artistic beauty that brings fantasy to life. As his wife says of him in the story's textual code: "Someone should go who could tell it well on returning. You have a way with words" (179). Indeed, the story, told through Bodoni's narrative focus, does "tell it well." More importantly, though, Bodoni "tells it well" to his children by creating the Mars trip as a reality through his unique ability to combine the imagination of his childhood with the maturity of his adulthood. Bodoni, by transforming his fantasy trip into reality, has created the artistic fantasy.

CONCLUSION

The Illustrated Man is more than a collection of short stories. It is a unified work with each story leading to the development of an overall theme. The collection is a *bildungsroman* of sorts since it depicts the artistic development of the un-named narrator. In order to make any valid conclusions about *The Illustrated Man* as a unified work, one must analyze the individual stories of the collection in relation to the narrative framework, the prologue and epilogue of the book. Since I have already given a plot synopsis of this framework in my introduction, I will now examine the prologue/epilogue in much the same manner as I have examined the individual stories, and relate discussions of individual stories to the analysis of this framework to show thematic unity.

The theme of fantasy and reality has been important in each of the stories we have examined so far. In the narrative framework, the narrator watches the Illustrated Man's fantasy pictures become reality, and each picture, in turn, depicts fantasy becoming reality. In the five stories I have examined, as well as in the narrative framework, a pattern emerges. In "The Veldt," children bring fantasy to life using technology coupled with their own primitive imaginations. The parents, in their rational adulthood, fail to see this possibility and are destroyed by the primitive fantasy. "Zero Hour" echoes this theme again as children bring a destructive fantasy to life with the help of alien beings and their own primitive imaginations. The adults, failing to see the possibility, are destroyed. "Kaleidoscope" again shows fantasy coming to life, though in a less sinister form. The adult, marooned in space and faced with certain death, makes a last wish that, in a small way, comes true with the help of a child. Again, the adult is destroyed, but at least something positive comes from his destruction. "The Long Rain" depicts how fantasy can be a delusion. The lieutenant finds the Sun Dome in his fantasy, yet his belief cannot make it a physical reality. Perhaps he is not child-like enough, and his adulthood makes it impossible to make that leap. The fantasy does become reality for him in his mind, however, and does ease his death and end his suffering. "The Rocket" presents a more optimistic view of fantasy becoming reality, and shows how a collaboration of imagination and experience can produce an artistic fantasy rather than a destructive one.

Each of these five stories, these five illustrations, teaches a lesson about fantasy becoming reality. The collection as a whole tells the story of a narrator-protagonist who watches the illustrations and learns their lessons. He learns how primitive fantasies can destroy those who do not accept them and take precautions; when he sees his own grim future forming on the Illustrated Man's back, he is prepared and saves himself from the primitive fantasy before it becomes real.

The stories also have another trait in common: they associate fantasy with children, or child-like thinking, and reality with adulthood, or rational thinking. The successful artist must learn to use both types of thinking in his work. The artist must "grow up," yet still retain a childish outlook on life in order to create and use his imagination. Or, as Freud has stated, "The creative writer does the same as the child at play. He creates a world of fantasy which he takes very seriously...." (749). Our narrator learns this artistic lesson by watching the illustrations; he then demonstrates his artistic ability by narrating the story of *The Illustrated Man*.

The Illustrated Man, then, shows the power of fantasy, or creation, while it warns us of its destructive potential. It is no secret that art can destroy as well as create; artists have a notorious history of self-destruction as the lives of Robert E. Howard, Edgar Allan Poe, Jimi Hendrix, Jim Morrison, Vincent Van Gogh, and scores of others can attest. Yet, when handled properly, man's creative powers can bring happiness and joy, as we see in "The Rocket."

The lessons of fantasy/reality and artistic creation

occur in the narrative framework as well as in each of the individual stories. In fact, the framework itself can be seen as a microcosm of the collection as a whole, since its success depends upon the same devices and themes that we have seen in the stories themselves.

As in each of the stories we have discussed so far, the narrative framework of *The Illustrated Man* relies heavily on the use of ellipses to create the cinematic effect of rapid movement from one scene to the next. The prologue consists of two scenes divided by an ellipsis on page 3. The first scene opens with the narrator's meeting the Illustrated Man and learning about his tattoos. The ellipsis transports the scene from afternoon to evening, just before bedtime. This begins the second scene, in which the narrator lies down and watches the illustrations. This scene ends with a final ellipsis—"The first Illustration quivered and came to life" (5), which makes the transition into the narratives of the individual illustrations. An ellipsis occurring after "The Veldt" transports the reader from one story to the next, "The Illustrated Man shifted in his sleep...."

(19), and a shorter one occurs in "Kaleidoscope" to remind us of the framework: "The Illustrated Man turned in the moonlight. He turned again... and again... and again..." (27). After this point, the framework does not intrude into the narrative until the epilogue, which begins somewhere near midnight. Each individual story, then, could be considered an ellipsis in itself since it transports the reader through an indefinite amount of time. As the narrator himself states, "Whether it took an hour or three hours for the dramas to finish, it would be hard to say" (4).

In *The Illustrated Man*, the ellipsis successfully creates the illusion of the cinema. This device is particularly effective in this collection because the reader (and the narrator) is supposedly *watching* the illustrations move and narrate their stories, rather than reading typewritten words on the printed page. The ellipsis allows Bradbury to quickly change camera angles and scenes, so to speak, even as the illustrations quickly change from one scene to the next: "The pictures were moving, each in its turn, each for a brief minute or two" (4).

The narrative framework, unlike the individual stories, is written in the first person point of view. This narrative focus is essential to the theme of the entire collection since the narrator tells his audience about an experience he has had, and from which, presumably, he has learned. The simple fact that the narrator makes the effort to tell this complex story shows that the Illustrated Man has influenced him in some important way. He must, then, tell his own story through his own point of view.

When he "fades out" into the individual stories themselves, Bradbury adopts a third person point of view that isolates the narrator from the stories. This third person focus resembles a camera as it transmits its cinematic narrative. Interestingly enough, however, the seventh story, "Rocket Man," is told through a first person focus, that of a young boy narrating his story. This first person viewpoint could not work in the first, second, or third story; since the reader would be too close to the narrative framework, the change in viewpoint would be distracting. By the seventh story, however, the illustrations have become so realistic, so alive, that the reader has forgotten about the framework. It is worthwhile to note that "Rocket Man" is narrated by a child—as we have seen, artistic creation requires a child-like imagination, and the proper narration of a story could certainly be considered artistic.

Bradbury obviously wants his reader to immerse himself in the individual tales. Changing narrative focus and eliminating transitions between all stories after the third tale helps to make the reader forget the framework while he concentrates on the stories themselves. Yet to understand the collection as a whole, we must not forget that we do not see the illustrations firsthand, but view them through the eyes of a narrator as he describes the tales. When this narrator first meets the Illustrated Man, he does not believe that fantasy can become real. After watching eighteen illustrations come to life, however, he believes and realizes both the creative power and the destructive potential of such a transformation. From these lessons he learns to tell us his experiences in such a way as to make a good story.

Throughout the framework of *The Illustrated Man*, Bradbury uses certain literary devices to achieve his meaning. As we have seen, the use of ellipses produces a cinematic technique that creates the illusion of moving pictures, and the narrative focus helps to elucidate the theme of narration and artistic creation. Examining the narrative framework in terms of Barthes' semiotic codes will reveal several additional themes that support this overall theme of fantasy becoming reality through artistic creation.

The cultural code of the narrative framework concerns the customs of society to avoid people who appear different from the norm. The Illustrated Man, because of his difference, must always live alone, shunned by others. Even casual friendships, such as his acquaintance with the narrator, cannot last. "You'll be sorry you asked me to stay," he tells the narrator (1).

The Illustrated Man is shunned because of his difference, yet his banishment from society runs deeper than this. The Illustrated Man, with his beautiful pictures, represents art—and, more importantly, artistic truth. The pictures, on one level, depict beauty; on a deeper level, however, they show truth, which is often ugly. People may claim to want truth, but they are usually unable to face it. The illustrations, fantasies, show that mankind is often ugly, evil, perverse, and miserable. Society cannot face such truths, even when painted in beautiful fantasies: they are still "windows looking in on fiery reality" (2). Instead, society ignores truth and the artist who displays it: "Everyone wants to see the pictures, and yet nobody wants to see them" (2).

The illustrations represent fantasy, yet they depict reality. In their beauty they show ugliness, which is truth. These conflicting descriptions of both the illustrations and the Illustrated Man form a theme of ambiguity that runs through the book as a whole. This ambiguity can be examined by applying Barthes' connotative code to the narrative framework.

The Illustrated Man, like his tattoos, represents an enigma as the narrator describes him with conflicting connotations. He is "tall, once well muscled" (1) with a "massive body" (1), yet "his face was like a child's" (1). He has a love-hate relationship with his own illustrations, it seems, as his hands move over them, preening them, "the motions of a connoisseur, an art patron" (4), while at the same time he states "I'd like to burn them off" (3). The Illustrated Man appears god-like—he is never actually named, yet his title is capitalized, as is the word "Illustration," and he appears virtually from nowhere, as if by magic. The narrator immediately finds himself in awe of the pictures, and their human canvas; however, this god-like creature is also described as tired (4), "going to fat" (1), and unable to sleep (4). The narrator, despite his awe, sees this stranger as mortal, after all, a tired, hungry man without a job.

The illustrations also show conflicting connotations. As we have seen, they show fantastic beauty even as they depict ugly realism. They are, in fact, a study in opposites: "Everyone wants to see the pictures, yet nobody wants to see them" (2). They are beautiful, yet terrible—"Any person would go a little mad with such things on his body," the narrator thinks (4). The illustrations, then, as well as their owner, project conflicting connotations that show their strangeness and mysteriousness, making them appear as the unexplained enigmas that they are.

One constant connotation personifies the Illustrations as living things (hence, the capital "I"): you could hear their voices murmuring... tiny mouths flickered... green and gold eyes winked, the tiny pink hands gestured" (2). The Illustrated Man himself says: "Sometimes at night I can feel them, the pictures, like ants crawling on my skin. Then I know they're doing what they have to do" (4). The pictures gain life by telling their stories—as we have seen in "Kaleidoscope," and earlier in this analysis of the framework, narration equals life. The narrator of *The Illustrated Man* lives to tell his tale, even as the Illustrations live; they, too, "tell a tale" according to their owner (3), and come to life through their narration: "The first Illustration quivered and came to life...." (5).

These living, moving pictures are contrasted with

the stillness that surrounds them. As soon as the Illustrated Man unveils his canvas, the pictures seem to move as they are "lurking among a constellation of freckles," or "peering from armpit caverns.... Each seemed intent upon his own activity" (2). We witness a gallery of motion: a "riot of rockets" (2), and "fountains of people" (2), all moving and alive. As the Illustrated Man states, "... the pictures move. The pictures change" (3).

If the pictures demonstrate life and movement, the human characters show stillness and inactivity. After the two men lie down for the night (4), the pictures begn their activity. The narrator, in particular, is hypnotized into stillness by this motion: "I lay fascinated and did not move while the stars wheeled in the sky" (5). The narrator, at this point, hovers close to death, like a mouse transfixed by the eyes of the serpent.

The epilogue immediately picks up this motion theme—the narrator still lies motionless as the last blank space on the Illustrated Man's back moves and comes to life to predict a possible future, a future that will become real if the narrator remains motionless and allows it to occur. But the narrator has learned the lessons of the eighteen Illustrations. He has seen the destructive nature of the uncontrolled fantasy, and has learned how to combine imagination and experience to create an artistic narrative. He knows the Illustrated Man and recognizes his possible madness and destructive potential. Because of these lessons, he does not remain motionless, like the parents in "The Veldt" and "Zero Hour." Instead, he acts: "I saw only enough of the Illustration to make me leap up.... I ran down the road in the moonlight" (186). The narrator knows that the illustrated nightmare *can* become real, and can destroy him.

With Barthes' symbolic code we can tie together the idea of fantasy/reality as a unifying theme in *The Illustrated Man* as a whole. In the framework, as in the entire collection, a thin line separates the two. The illustrations represent fantasy, works of art. Yet they are also "windows looking in upon fiery reality" (2) that predict the future and show us what will become real. The pictures, the fantasies, transform and become reality, as we have seen throughout the collection. The Illustrations are destructive in their transformation. The narrator takes these pictures, however, and uses imagination and experience to neutralize their destructiveness and he transforms them into artistic reality. Metaphorically, then, Bradbury himself transforms fantasy into reality by creating *The Illustrated Man*.

The framework, then, becomes a sort of textual code for the collection as a whole as the narrator speaks of the artistic lessons he has learned in the stories themselves. Each story, in essence, reinforces the theme of artistic creation, the theme that our narrator (and, presumably, Bradbury himself) has learned in order to produce the narrative. The narration becomes self-reflective, then, on the subject of narration.

I first read *The Illustrated Man* many years ago, before I became a student of literature and literary theory. I was a child, then, filled with wonder and imagination—the stories entertained me and appealed to my sense of wonder. Somehow, I, like the narrator of the collection, have learned the lessons of the eighteen stories. Enough of the child lives within me to still enjoy the tales as journeys into the imagination. The adult part of me, though, has learned about literature, its theory, structure, and technique. I have the best of both worlds, then, as does Ray Bradbury. I can see the themes and literary techniques within the collection, yet I can still retain enough imagination to enjoy what I've read. And Bradbury, "the man with the child inside who remembers all" (*Stories* xiii), can utilize his experience to create serious literature, while using his imagination to create stories that appeal to the sense of wonder of the reading public.

WORKS CITED

Barthes, Roland. *S/Z*. Trans. Richard Miller. New York: Hill and Wang, 1974. Print.

—. *Image Music Text*. Trans Stephen Heath. New York: Hill and Wang, 1979. Print.

—. "Textual Analysis of Poe's 'Valdemar'." *Untying the Text*. Ed. Robert Young. Boston: Routledge & Kegan Paul, 1981. Print.

Bradbury, Ray. *The Illustrated Man*. New York: Bantam, 1969. Print.

—. *The Stories of Ray Bradbury*. New York: Knopf, 1980. Print.

Freud, Sigmund. "Creative Writers and Daydreaming." *Critical Theory Since Plato*. Ed. Hazard Adams. New York: Harcourt Brace Jovanovich, 1971. Print.

Genette, Gerard. *Figures of Literary Discourse*. Trans. Alan Sheridan. New York: Columbia University

Press, 1982. Print.

—. *Narrative Discourse*. Trans. Jane E. Lewin. Ithica: Cornell University Press, 1982. Print.

Klein, T. E. D. "Horrors!: An Introduction to Writing Horror Fiction." *The Secrets of Writing Popular Fiction*. Cinncinati: Writer's Digest Publications, 1986. Print.

Kubler-Ross, Elisabeth. *On Death and Dying*. New York: Macmillan, 1970. Print.

Rico, Gabriele Lusser. *Writing the Natural Way*. Los Angeles: J. P. Tarcher, 1983. Print.

Scholes, Robert. *Semiotics and Interpretation*. New Haven: Yale University Press, 1982. Print.

—.*Structural Fabulation: An Essay on Fiction of the Future*. Notre Dame: University of Notre Dame Press, 1975. Print.

—. *Structuralism in Literature*. New Haven: Yale University Press, 1974. Print.

Todorov, Tzvetan. *The Fantastic: A Structural Approach to a Literary Genre*. Cleveland: Case Western University, 1973. Print.

—. *Poetics of Prose*. Ithica: Cornell University Press, 1977. Print

APPENDIX
DICTIONARY OF SYMBOLS

A= adult   -= neg of trait   opt= wishes

C= child   >= leads to   cre= creates

D= death   thru= through   des= destroys

F= fantasy   ( )= "offstage"   tra= travels

Fm= family   [ ]= possibility   R= reality

H= happiness   += achieves/wins   Rk= rocket

Sp= space   bel= believes   S= success

P= power   sks= seeks   Pl= plays

Equations

"The Veldt":

C- opt R> C opt F> C cre F> A opt des F> F bec R> F des A> C bec A> C opt R

"Kaleidoscope":

A-S> A opt S> A sks S thru Sp> A-H> Sp des Rk> A opt H> Sp des A> A cre H thru C> F bec R. A+S thru D

"The Long Rain":

A-H> A opt H> A cre H thru F> A+H (D thru F)

"Zero Hour":

C-P> C opt P> C pl F> A-bel F> F bec R (F des A> C+P

"The Rocket":

A-H> A opt F> [A+F> Fm-H]> A-F> A+Rk> A cre F

thru Rk> F bec R> Fm+F> A+F> A+F> A+H

CLASSIFICATION OF THE STORIES OF *THE ILLUSTRATED MAN*

Although space limitations prevent a detailed analysis of each of the stories, the entire eighteen tales may be classified as follows:

The Destructive Fantasy

"The Veldt": examined in detail in the main text.

"The Highway": man's ability to destroy himself through science.

"The Rocket Man": a completely opposite view from that of "Kaleidoscope." The rocket man's d e a t h, rather than being redemptive, destroys his family. Furthermore, the rocket man is mesmerized by space, just as the narrator is mesmerized by the illustrations. The rocket man cannot break this spell and is destroyed.

"Last Night of the World": a dream becomes real, leading to the destruction of the world.

"The Fox and the Forest": the future world in this story represents the destructive potential of man. The characters try to escape from this fantasy by returning to the past, a fantasy of its own. Yet this past fantasy, which is actually a past reality, cannot save them.

"The Visitor": a man who has the power to make fantasy become reality is destroyed by others who lack his artistic vision.

"Concrete Mixer": Martian invaders are destroyed by the American dream, a fantasy that has gone out of control.

"Marionettes, Inc.": a man creates a fantasy in his own

image and it destroys him.

"The City": this city is similar to "The Veldt" and "Marionettes, Inc."—again, man's fantasy ultimately destroys him.

"Zero Hour": examined in detail in the man text.

The Redemptive Fantasy

"Kaleidoscope": examined in detail in the main text.

"The Other Foot": a fantasy of revenge becomes redemptive after the characters are shown the consequences of the destructive fantasy.

"The Man": one man finds the redemptive fantasy while another man fails to see it, even though it is right before his eyes.

"The Fire Balloons": the aliens represent the fantasy of perfection, freedom, and immortality. They have become free of sin through the redemptive fantasy.

The Self-Delusional Fantasy

"No Particular Night or Morning": the protagonist is destroyed because he is unable to believe in anything, fantasy or reality. He becomes so delusional that fantasy and reality become confused and he cannot believe either.

"The Long Rain": examined in detail in the main text.

The Artistic Fantasy

"The Exiles": the artistic fantasy is destroyed by an audience who lacks the imagination to appreciate it.

"The Rocket": examined in detail in the main text.

ABOUT THE AUTHOR

James Arthur Anderson teaches English and Literature at Johnson & Wales University's North Miami Campus, where he holds the rank of Professor. He has a B.A. and M.A. from Rhode Island College, and a Ph.D. from the University of Rhode Island. He is the author of *Out of the Shadows: a Structuralist Approach to Understanding the Fiction of H. P. Lovecraft*, and a horror novel *The Altar*, also published by The Borgo Press. His critical articles have appeared in *Lovecraft Studies*, *Crypt of Cthulhu*, *Studies in Weird Fiction*, and *Clio: a Journal of Literature, History, and the History of Literature*.

Dr. Anderson's fiction has appeared in *Horrors!: 365 Scary Stories*; *Swords Against Darkness V*; *Weird Tales 4*; and *Eldritch Tales*. He lives in South Florida with his wife Lynn and enjoys riding his Paso Fino horse *Ilución de Contrallano.*

www.ingramcontent.com/pod-product-compliance
Lightning Source LLC
LaVergne TN
LVHW041626070426
835507LV00008B/477